EVERYDAY SUCHNESS

Buddhist Essays on Everyday Living

Gyomay M. Kubose

Dharma House Publishing
Coarsegold, California
2025

Copyright © 1967 G.M. Kubose
Bright Dawn Center of Oneness Buddhism
Fourteenth printing 2025

All rights reserved.
No part of this book may be used
or reproduced in any manner whatsoever without
written permission from the rights holder/publisher.

14th Edition was made possible by
the generous support of the
Bright Dawn Lay Minister Council and the Kubose Family.

Cover design by neko
Photo credit: Ryoan-ji, Kyoto by Cquest
www.commons.wikimedia.org CC BY-SA 2.5

DHARMA HOUSE PUBLISHING
28372 Margaret Road
Coarsegold, CA 93614
info@brightdawn.org

ISBN 978-0-9642992-6-9
ISBN 0-9642992-6-7

Printed in the United States of America

Dedicated to my teacher Reverend Haya Akegarasu

FORWARD TO THE 14th EDITION

Everyday Suchness is a collection of short essays written by Rev. Gyomay Kubose during the first 20 years or so of his tenure at the Buddhist Temple of Chicago, which he founded in 1945. It was first published in 1967, which was a watershed year in Western culture.

A lot has happened since then, including at least a dozen printings of this book. As inventory was depleted and the publishing folks started preparing to print more—including converting the text to digital—we saw this as an opportunity to enhance the content by adding some context to Rev. Kubose's excellent and timeless dharma teachings.

Rev. Kubose—nee Masao Kubose—was born in 1905 in San Francisco. When he was 2 ½ years old, he was sent to live with his father's parents in Japan. He grew up on their farm not far from Hiroshima and attended agricultural school. After graduating, he decided that rather than farming and teaching in Japan, he would return to the US and continue his studies.

In 1922, he returned to California. Soon afterward, he attended a memorial service at the Oakland Buddhist Church, where he had his first real contact with Buddhism. Recognizing Masao's budding interest in Buddhism, the minister gave him some pamphlets written by Rev. Haya Akegarasu. Those teachings had a profound impact on him, and at age 24, he accompanied Akegarasu on a tour of the US.

After receiving a degree in Philosophy from the University of California, Berkeley in 1936, the newlywed Masao and his wife, Minnie, left for Japan to join Akegarasu. Soon after arriving at the temple, Rev. Akegarasu ordained Masao and gave him the dharma name, Gyomei. (He later changed the spelling to make it easier for Americans to pronounce).

In the next few years, Japan became increasingly embroiled in military conflicts in the region. It soon became clear Japan was not going to be a safe place for Americans—including Gyomay and Minnie. They left Japan and arrived back in California on July 4, 1941.

A few months after the bombing of Pearl Harbor, the Kubose family and more than 120,000 Japanese Americans were ordered to leave the west coast. They eventually arrived at an internment camp in Heart Mountain, Wyoming. They stayed there until 1944, with Rev. Kubose leading Buddhist services at an altar built out of scrap lumber.

In 1944, the Kubose family left Wyoming for Chicago, where about 20,000 Japanese from the internment camps had settled. By January 1945, he had financed the purchase of a boarded-up church in the Hyde Park neighborhood and began holding services at the Chicago Buddhist Church, which later became the Buddhist Temple of Chicago.

As part of his ministry there, Rev. Kubose wrote articles for its newsletter. Those essays became the nucleus for this book. These essays are dharma teachings—their purpose is to embody and relay the Buddha's teachings. However, Rev. Kubose's approach to the dharma was unique, which probably explains why this book and its successors have been read by so many people.

Unlike many dharma teachers, Rev. Kubose didn't just talk and write about "things the Buddha said to monks." Rather, he believed the dharma should be applied to life—real, everyday life as experienced by ordinary human beings living in the world of jobs, households, and relationships. Most of these short essays deal with the spirituality of what he calls the "little things" in life and the importance of greeting life as it is in all its Suchness.

However, during the years between 1945 and 1967, the real everyday lives of Rev. Kubose and his congregation were affected by a massive wave of social change. The reader will likely notice references to issues like race and gender, and may occasionally wonder where Rev. Kubose's dharma legacy stands on such issues.

During the years following the second World War, a massive Civil Rights Movement began, born out of frustration with racial segregation and discrimination. Other social movements sought, among other things, to equalize treatment of individuals based on gender, ban nuclear weapons, and eliminate discrimination and police harassment based on sexual identity.

In 1967, much of this activity came to a head. In San Francisco, thousands of young people converged on San Francisco for the Summer of Love, a countercultural phenomenon that blended opposition to the war in Vietnam with friendliness toward equal rights, spiritual awakening, and psychedelic drugs.

This was also the Long Hot Summer, when frustration over racial injustice and police brutality sparked riots in many US cities. The antiwar movement escalated in October when demonstrators against the Vietnam War rioted at the Pentagon. Meanwhile, the National Organization for Women (NOW) added reproductive rights to its Women's Bill of Rights, and the Gay Liberation Movement coalesced around protests against police harassment.

Against this backdrop of chaos and division, Rev. Kubose guided, with kindness to everyone, the organization he established. Thus he generously offered the Buddha-dharma to many Japanese Americans and a growing number of other Americans.

While these essays don't promote any partisanship, readers will notice that Rev. Kubose didn't shy away from these issues, either. However, as the Lotus Sutra says, the dharma rain falls on all plants in the forest, regardless of their appearance or purpose.

When the Buddhist Temple of Chicago celebrated its 30th Anniversary, Rev. Kubose outlined his dream of establishing a uniquely American Buddhism, one that "can be explained in simple, everyday language and practiced in everyday life," but is still uniquely Buddhist, and non-dualistic, and that will "bring about a peaceful, meaningful, creative life, both individually and collectively."

A few years later, his son and dharma heir, Rev. Koyo Sunnan Kubose, began working with his father to carry out this vision, transcribing talks and publishing more books. In 1996, they founded a nonprofit organization for the purpose, which eventually became Bright Dawn Center of Oneness Buddhism.

Rev. Gyomay Kubose passed away in March 2000. Rev. Koyo Kubose passed away in March 2022. However, the Kubose dharma legacy continues in the form of Bright Dawn Center of Oneness Buddhism, which now operates from Coarsegold, California. The organization is governed by a Board of Directors, with day to day activities overseen by a Leadership Council.

Besides continuing to publish books and newsletters, Bright Dawn conducts a program to train Lay Ministers in his Way of Oneness. As of this writing, about 150 people have completed the LM program. They are inducted into the Buddhist clergy, but not as monastics—rather, an LM maintains "householder" status in order to embody the "everyday dharma" that Kubose offered.

Occasionally, an LM-in-training will read *Everyday Suchness* and question a perhaps-outdated reference to gender or the like. Again, bear in mind these essays were written during a time of great social change, and many people observed longstanding social traditions which have since evolved.

Bright Dawn still does not endorse political candidates or parties. However, it is a diverse organization, intentionally free from ideas like rank and status—and with no distinction about race, gender, or any of those other identities society likes to use as dividing lines. The Kubose dharma legacy embodies the Way of Oneness—and "otherness" just doesn't fit in.

Morris Sekiyo Sullivan

PREFACE

For some time I have been asked to publish in book form the articles which I have written in the past years. However, I did not have an opportunity to do so. To mark my sixtieth birthday a few of my friends practically forced me to get the publication on its way. Mr. William Gilbert, president of The American Buddhist Association, took the initiative and selected the articles. In response to the wishes of many of my friends, I have finally decided to publish these articles which are honest footsteps of my spiritual growth. At this time I want to express my appreciation to all those who have urged and helped me to publish this book.

Now that this book is finally going to be published, I feel as if my own child is going out into the world. I hope that you will extend your life's friendship to this little life's messenger; so that we will find ourselves in the world of suchness to enjoy together the worthiness and serenity of life.

It seems that the little things are important in our life. In fact our life is made up of little things. They make life spark just as a pinch of salt makes the food taste better, or a drop of oil makes a machine run smoothly. If through this book joy and serenity are found and a meaning to life is discovered, the purpose of this book will be fulfilled.

I would like to dedicate this book to my most dear and reverent teacher, the late Rev. Haya Akegarasu, to whom my whole life is dedicated, because without meeting him I would have never found Buddhism nor myself. I feel that I came into this world just to meet my teacher who gave me my name Gyomay which means bright dawn.

G.M. Kubose
February 22, 1967

CONTENTS

Forward to the 14th Edition i

Preface vii

Introduction xi

Happiness 1

Awareness 7

Limitations 11

Is Your Switch On? 17

Gautama Buddha 19

Thoughts for the New Year 25

Story of a Crutch 29

Selflessness 32

The Mind's Eye 36

Honesty 45

Right Understanding 47

Healthful Outlook Toward Life and Death 50

Beyond the Relative World 54

Buddhism, Zen, and Nembutsu 57

Reality of Brotherhood 63

Non-dichotomization 66
The Greatest Gift to Mother 74
Introspections 78
Non-Attachment 81
The Life of Becoming 84
Freedom 89
Living Life 93
Naturalness 96
Serenity 99
Nirvana 103
Life without Regret 107
The Center of Life 109
Eternal Present 111
Oneness 113
Beautify the Mind 115
Is Life Fun? 117
Water 120
A Stone 122

INTRODUCTION

EDITOR'S NOTE: This was written in 1967 by William Gilbert, who spearheaded the book's production. Gilbert also helped establish the American Buddhist Association (ABA), which formed at the Buddhist Temple of Chicago in 1955. Gilbert served as the ABA president for a number of years. The organization has since ceased operation, although similar associations formed as Buddhism spread throughout the US and the West.

This collection of articles is destined to become a personal treasury for the many people who have already had the good fortune to have read them. They are the work of a man who many feel exemplifies the living spirit of Buddhism in all its aspects of universality.

Gyomay M. Kubose is the head minister of the Buddhist Temple of Chicago which he founded in 1944 in the aftermath of the Japanese relocation. He has been cited many times for his work in the field of brotherhood and community relations, and he is also the recipient of the highest honors in the Boy Scout movement. Rev. Kubose's services are constantly in demand as a speaker at mid-western universities, civic groups and religious congregations. His many accomplishments are too numerous to mention but let it suffice to say that his is best known as one of those rare individuals; a complete human being with an insight into the true meaning of life that is superb and incomparable.

These short articles are a regular feature of his temple bulletin and for a long time, many people have urged him to have a select group published in book form, so they could share this wonderfully fresh attitude with other people.

What is Suchness? It is things as they are and life as it is. It is truth as it is. Suchness is the world, void of artificiality or make-up. It is "Sonomama" in Japanese and "Tathata" in Sanskrit. A rose is a rose; a lily is a lily; and I am I. This is the world of Suchness!

He points out that true happiness consists in identifying oneself with something that transcends mere instinctive urges. That one's well-being consists in leaving behind the separate, fearful, self-centered individual we often find ourselves to be, and become one with the universal and absolute reality. The essence of these articles is liberation from attachment to the demands and desires that hold us captive; and to the shrinking self that erects a protective wall of separation between ourselves and other forms of life.

The greatest truths have always been the most simple. So simple are they, that at first we find ourselves unable to grasp their real significance. In this book, Kubose succeeds in transmitting the essence of Buddhistic thought—of life itself, with the remarkable elements of simplicity and clarity that is the mark of every great teacher. He holds forth the possibility of a serene, perfectly clear, harmonious and relaxed mental life. To those of us who have had the good fortune to have been associated with him, his message is both strong and clear. The role of transcendental wisdom consists not in conditioning the human mind, but in liberating it.

William Gilbert

"Oneness"

Rev G M Kubeka

HAPPINESS

All men, without exception, wish to have a happy life, and they work hard to attain it. To gain freedom and equality means, in the end, to live a happy life. Many wars have been fought for this prize. It seems as if all human history is the history of the struggle for the attainment of happiness. All our plans are directed to this end, and all our energies are spent to attain it. It seems happiness is the ultimate goal of life. Let us examine what this happiness is, that all of us seek, and the way to happiness that everyone is looking for.

What is happiness? We must know clearly what the objective is when we seek it. If we do not know, our effort may be in vain. The ancient Greeks thought that good is happiness. But in the middle and modern ages, Aristotle's formal meaning that good is happiness has been altered to the more material meaning that happiness is pleasure or absence of pain. John Stuart Mill says in his Utilitarianism: "By happiness is intended pleasure and the absence of pain; by unhappiness, pain and the absence of pleasure." He gives qualitative differences in pleasure. John Dewey distinguishes between happiness and pleasure by saying that happiness is permanent and universal and is a feeling of the whole self, while pleasure is transitory and relative and is a feeling of some aspect of self. Aristotle says the good of man, the happiness, is an activity of the soul in accordance with excellence; or, if there are more excellences than one, in accordance with the best and most perfect excellence. Spinoza says happiness is not the reward of virtue but virtue itself.

In Sanskrit happiness is called sukha. Sukha includes both the relatively static state that we name happiness or felicity, and the conscious moments of such a state to which our psychology refers as pleasurable or pleasant feeling. Sukha is applied alike to physical health, material well-being, and spiritual beatitude. In Buddhism feeling is divided into three: sukha, happiness; dukha, pain; and adukhamasukha, neutral feeling. The neutral feeling is identical with happiness, namely, happiness of the loftier kind. The pleasures and happiness arising from the five senses we call the happiness of worldly desires. The loftier kind of joy arises in connection with the practice of dhyana, meditation. In the last stage of dhyana, all positive feeling, joy or melancholy, is merged in neutral feeling or indifference; perfect clarity of mind is attained and ignorance is banished, so that consciousness is in complete equanimity and clarity of mind. Sidgwick says that Buddhist happiness is universalistic hedonism because it is neither egoistic nor altruistic. Buddha's mission was not only to overcome ill but to attain the good and happiness of all beings: happiness-bringing for self and others. In Buddhism the striving toward a goal is happiness, as compared with the Indian ascetics who sacrifice everything for a goal.

Now, to bring the subject closer to our daily life. We attain happiness in various ways in our daily life. However, we can divide it into three—physical, material, and spiritual. By physical I mean that one is happy because he is healthy, handsome or beautiful. Materially, one is happy because he (or she) is rich, lives in a nice home, owns a beautiful car, has many clothes, jewels, and plenty of good food. Mental and spiritual happiness is in friendship and love. Happiness is created when one is honored, praised, sympathized with, comforted, etc.

These conditions of happiness depend on external causes. Happiness is attained by possessing something or being given something by someone. Therefore, when the cause of the happiness is gone or destroyed, the happiness also disappears. It is beyond our control. Let us take some examples. Your physical happiness: you are young and beautiful, and handsome, and you are healthy and strong. Indeed, you are happy and thankful. But suppose you have an accident and become crippled, or you become sick. Your happiness cannot depend on your health. Of course, your beauty and strength will fade away with the passing of time. Therefore, health, beauty, and strength are not to be depended on for real eternal happiness, though they are important factors in our happiness. We have to attain a way of happiness other than the physical, so that we can enjoy life, and be happy and appreciative even though we are sick, or aged, or crippled.

Kenko, a famous Buddhist priest and author of "Tsurezuregusa," once said, "It is not worthwhile having a friend who has never had the experience of illness." A person so healthy that he has never been sick does not understand the real meaning of sympathy and kindness. One who is so healthy tends to become stubborn and to create friction and trouble. In this case, health is not a source of happiness but of trouble. Also, it is evident that material happiness is uncertain and undependable. In this age of mammonism, money is everything. People believe that the almighty dollar can buy anything and everything. True, money is very important in this pecuniary-conscious world. But happiness that is bought with money vanishes when the money is gone. Money brings happiness, but at the same time money brings misery. So money is not the way of happiness. A beautiful car, a fine home, good food, fine clothing, and other belongings are in the same category. They are important and will bring happiness, but they are undependable and uncertain; and many times they bring suffering through destruction, theft, or envy. Even the happiness brought by love, friendship, sympathy and the kindness of friends cannot be depended on, for love often becomes hate, and friends become enemies, because they are all relative. Happiness that is brought by physical, material, and mental means is attained through external causes. That is the very reason they are undependable. Therefore, we should look for internal rather than external causes of happiness.

Buddhism teaches us to look into the core of things, instead of looking around. We have to look within ourselves to see what creates happiness. For instance, TO BE LOVED is happiness, but TO LOVE also is happiness. It is happy to receive something; but also to give and share is happiness. The happiness of the giver is more permanent and rich than that of the recipient. In the spirit of real giving and sharing, and loving, there is no limit. The happiness is the loving or sharing itself, and not necessarily the result. The real enjoyment of work is the working itself rather than the result of the work. Real happiness is not the happiness that is received from without but that which is created within. Modern people in general are result seekers. Their attitude is that if they will get some benefit they will do something; but if there is no profit, what is the use? The result seekers are profit seekers. In other words, modern people think the end is more important than the means. Someone has said that two modern ideologies are represented by Stalin and Gandhi: Gandhi's way is that the means are as important as the end, while for Stalin the end is so important that the end justifies the means. Buddhists are taught that every step and every means are very important. Every means itself is an end. For artists, musicians, and sculptors the work itself is pleasure and happiness, but for moneymakers work is only the means to make money. Work is pain and suffering, and the suffering is to be compensated by the spending of money: this is modern life. I feel very sorry for people who live this type of life. The most happy and fortunate person is he who enjoys his work besides earning money.

    The real way of happiness is the realization of one's life itself. It is the unfolding of the whole self. The real way of happiness is in the way of giving, rather than happiness in receiving. We must find the way of love rather than that of being loved. It is the life of always giving, loving, sharing, and the enjoyment of work that is always creative and has no end, while the other ways of happiness turn into failure or disappointment. True happiness is not given to us—we create it. If you are unhappy, do not blame others or your environment. It is your mind, your attitude, that make you miserable. Changing place, or work, may help, but that is not the complete cure for your trouble and unhappiness. The right attitude, and a clear and right mind are the way to happiness.

AWARENESS

It is said a Buddhist's life is a life of awareness. I have just read one of the finest examples of this life of awareness in a magazine I receive each month from Japan called "Taiko" (or "Great Cultivation" in English). The Editor is Sumita Oyama, and in this month's issue he has written of a very beautiful life. I was so inspired by it that I should like to share it with you.

When the Russian scientists shot the intercontinental ballistic missile and took a picture of the other side of the moon, Mr. Oyama's awareness of this incident was: "Well, the Russians took a picture of the other side of the moon. Really, the moon is round and there is no front side or back side. Things we call front or back are man-made ideas. The moon has no back or front. At any rate, the Russians took a picture of the back of the moon." Then he continues, "I wish Khrushchev himself would take a picture of the other side of his own mind when he speaks to the leaders of the world. Well, it's his business, but how about myself? I think I should clean the back of my house." So he started to clean the back of his house, his backyard.

Man in general has a front and a back. Of course, we want to present a beautiful front and keep all other things in the back. Mr. Oyama quotes a haiku (a 17-syllable Japanese poem) by the great Buddhist poet and monk, Ryokan:

"*Ura wo mise, omote wo misete, chiru momiji.*"

Translated, this is;
Showing front,
Showing back,
Maple leaves fall.

We try to put up a nice front; that is why we have problems. There is really no front and back in true life. We should live as the maple leaves, showing both front and back. Front is front and back is back, but there is no superiority to either side. Both are true. But we petty human beings try to show the "better" front and hide the back. If we were able to take pictures of our own minds, front and back, if we were able to live life as the maple leaves, showing the front as front and back as back, there would be no falseness, no pretense, no secrets to hide— show ourselves to the world, live our life. We, most of us, consciously and unconsciously, live a life of front and back duplicity. And that is the trouble today, the very foundation of perplexity in life.

This is what Ryokan was concerned about. He wanted to live life like a maple leaf by showing front and back as they are —with no shamefulness, just straightforward honesty and sincerity in life. As soon as we think, "This side is better to show the public; this should be hidden," then we have problems. A Buddhist life is a life of this honesty. There is no front and no back. A true life is totality. This side of the hand or that side of the hand—is one better or worse? This side is this side; that side is that side. Both are equal. Nothing to be hidden.

Mr. Oyama, when he read the news about taking a picture of the other side of the moon, became aware of the many sides of our own life. He was living a life of awareness. There are hundreds of such teachings around us every day. But how many of us, when we read this news, would have thought of this front and back of our own mind and our own life? Mr. Oyama, with his idea of front and back, gives a wonderful teaching and wonderful way of awareness in his article.

As I read this article, it struck me how true it is that there is no front and back, but that we are the ones who make front and back, left and right, east and west. It is our mind which creates this front and back, just as we create our own problems. So live a life like a maple leaf, showing the back as well as the front, and do not be bothered by showing only a front or back. There is no front or back; both are good. This kind of awareness is, I think, a Buddhist's life.

I was visiting a friend in a hospital. We talked about acceptance. Acceptance is very important in life. In the English language, however, acceptance has the connotation of a defeated attitude: "Well, it's something I can't help, so I have to accept it." "Well, there is something better than this, but since it came to me, I can't help it. I just have to accept it." The true attitude in Buddhism is not such an attitude of defeatedness. Acceptance means understanding of the truth, accepting the fact. Accepting the truth means a true understanding of life—not the feeling of a victim, not a feeling of sacrifice or being defeated—but understanding the true facts about life. Then from here, our true life begins. Without accepting things as they are, without knowing the truth—what it is, what I am—then true life does not begin. The acceptance of true life as I am, as you are, or the conditions in which you are, the true realization of the fact, is acceptance. Instead of becoming a victim of the conditions or whatever it is, you become the master of the situation. This is acceptance. Acceptance has a very positive, active, dynamic meaning in Buddhism, and not the defeated, negative sense as implied in the English language.

Know the fact. The fact is that there is no front and back, so we can be honest to ourselves. There is nothing to hide when we are sincere and honest. "Maple leaves falling off by showing front and back." I can see the falling maple leaves, turning in the autumn sun, showing front and back as they come down. It is a natural life. No pretense, no worry, no tension. Just as a maple leaf falls, as water falls from a higher level, just as the moon shines—that kind of life gives us peace and serenity. And this is awareness. The teachings are around us only when we are aware. Mr. Sumita Oyama surely has great awareness in his living. I greatly admire this man and so wanted to share his life of awareness and introspection with you.

LIMITATIONS

The first teaching of Buddha was to know thyself. He taught that the most important thing in solving your problems is to know yourself first. This idea was not his own creation. A Greek philosopher, Socrates, taught the same thing. In another way of expressing it, it seems to me that to know oneself is to know one's limitations. I do not mean "limitations" in the ordinary sense. It is not limiting yourself. This "limitations" is not a correct word, perhaps. By "to know your own limitations," I mean to know what you are.

I think psychological problems, neurotic difficulties, are the result of failure to realize one's own limitations. Perhaps "appropriateness" or "position" is a better word. One's limitation in a society or in a family is one's position. It is what you can do, what you should do, in the most appropriate capacity. Limitation does not limit your action, speech or thought. It is knowing what you are and living accordingly.

A limitation is not a set thing. Especially, appropriate position in society must be varied according to the context of the situation and what you are doing. The only limitation of the rose is that it cannot be a lily. Since the rose does not care, it is no limitation.

Similarly, the children's position as related to the parents—there is a definite place—the teacher's position, student's position, wife and husband's—the husband has his own position to fulfill, just as the wife has her own position to fulfill. This sense of limitation is not in knowing limits: "Well, I cannot do this; I am not good enough," and so on—not in that sense, but to be free to exercise one's fullest capability and unfold the fullest extent of one's ability. But to be able to do this, to be so free, one should know one's limitations. You can see that this meaning of limitation is more than the ordinary sense.

But even in the ordinary sense: A person is frustrated because he thinks he deserves a higher wage for his work, but to the eye of an employer, he does not, as he has only the ability to perform certain things. We sometimes expect more money for less work. Or we try to do a thing which is beyond our own capabilities. Or someone expects more from us than we can do. Such unfair expectations by ourselves or from others are a cause of many modern diseases.

Once a great conductor of the Russian Chorus was asked by his wife, "Dear, don't you think I could be the best ballet dancer in the Imperial Russian Ballet Troupe?" The husband immediately replied, "It is not a question of you being the best in the ballet troupe. In a fine line of dancers, the small part is

LIMITATIONS

just as important as being the star of the group." When one wants to be the best in a group (instead of the best that one is) and forgets one's own ability, there is frustration and blaming of others: "They don't give me a chance," "There's something wrong with the leader."

In not understanding our own limitations, we sometimes underestimate our ability or we sometimes overestimate our ability, and either way, we are unrealistic about our expectations. Of course, this is concerned with the teaching of the middle way.

A child should know his limitations as a child; this is a very important thing. Not to limit oneself, but to be free and to do all one can. One should know what he is, what his position is, what his ability is. Buddha's teaching was this: to know one's own position in a designated time, place, and occasion. Many times we fail to see our own limitations; we expect praise and if it does not come, we feel miserable. Or there is a person with real ability, yet he thinks, "Oh, I cannot do it." Inferiority complex creeps in; there is perplexity in his life. So Buddha's teaching, "to know yourself first" is the most important teaching in modern life.

Of course, many of us believe that we are all good, that we are doing our share. The other day I heard a very interesting story. There was a very particular housewife who was very capable in keeping house, keeping her kitchen in order and her backyard clean; and she was also a good gardener, and so on. She was very proud of herself for being so capable in maintaining her household. One afternoon, a friend visited her and while they sat in the kitchen talking of many things, this lady said, "Mary, do you see my neighbor next door? She is such an untidy worker, just look at her laundry—how dirty it is, there are spots on her sheets and it looks as if they hadn't been washed, and her garden isn't kept up, etc." The visiting friend then said, "Well, Margaret, maybe that's true, but I think if you will wash your window, your neighbor's sheets and yard will look much cleaner."

We have the same kind of faulty outlook on other people. We think we are good and doing fine but that others are not. Really, when we look at ourselves, we are not ones to be too proud as compared to others.

Here is another old story told in Japan—about a devout churchgoer, a very conscientious, religious man, and his son who had been graduated from the university and knew all about modern science. To this young son, going to church was nonsense. He was always against his father going to church and constantly asked why he went to church, especially when the minister did not seem to practice what he preached. The young son practically insisted that his father should not go to church. The father said, "Son, you don't understand what spiritual life is." But he could not convince his son, so he came up with a new idea—that of an agreement, and he said, "I will quit going to church if you will promise to do these things for me: For the next two weeks, I want you to keep a diary of all the things you have said, all the things you have thought, and all the things you have done. At the end of the two weeks, please show me the diary. If you can write these things very honestly and sincerely for two weeks and I can see the diary, I will quit going to church."

"Oh, Dad, that's easy enough. I will do exactly as you ask." The son kept the diary honestly and sincerely, and put down all the things his father had mentioned. But after one week when he read his own diary, he immediately realized that he was ashamed to show it to other people. Everything of his private life was in the diary. Because of his shame, he came to his father and said, "Dad, I am going to quit keeping the diary. I cannot do it any more. All the things that I had put down I am ashamed to show to others—even to you. You know, I thought I was good, that I was doing everything fine, but when I became frankly honest with myself—writing down all the things I have done privately, have said privately, and have thought to myself—I found that I just could not show it to you or anyone else."

"Well, you see, son, we all think we are good and that there is nothing to be ashamed of, but if we strip ourselves and look into our own ego self, we are very selfish and we do a lot of things we do not want other people to know about. That is the very reason I go to church. I go in order to look into myself, for that true inner peace that comes from self-introspection, and, as for myself, for the first time I am able to forgive or understand other people's faults and shortcomings. It is so easy to accuse others, blame others, but when we inspect ourselves, we are the same—we are not angels, either."

For the first time, the young son realized why his father

went to church—not to show religiousness or to listen to the sermons, but for his own introspection and to make his inner peace.

When we look externally and criticize others or imitate others without knowing our own limitations, we always have trouble. There is no inner peace in ourselves. I think that is the purpose of going to church. Going to church is not learning what Buddha said or what is said in books, but being able to see what we are and living our own life according to its own limitations. These limitations include the fullest capacity or ability or potentiality. We go to church to listen to lectures—what for? Not to gain knowledge, but to deepen our self-introspection and widen our scope of understanding. If we understand ourselves, we have no right to blame others—we understand them. Only through understanding do we have peace and harmony. That kind of approach is what Buddha taught. It eliminates mental agony, anger, stubbornness, and greediness. All these can be eliminated or transcended by understanding ourselves. This is what I mean by knowing one's own limitations or one's position.

IS YOUR SWITCH ON?

When the switch is on, current flows; it lights up a room or turns a motor. No matter how good the motor may be and how large a lamp may be, unless the switch is on the devices are useless. They are lifeless.

Air is filled with sound waves of good lectures, music and pictures, but unless you have a receiving set, you do not receive them. Even though you have a perfect radio and television set, unless you turn on the switch nothing happens. There is no music and no picture. Turning on the switch is the most important. So in life to turn on the switch in our life is the most essential for a worthwhile and a truly joyous life.

We want to live and not merely exist. To live means a meaningful, worthwhile and joyous life and not just physically existing. We eat, sleep, and work, but unless we turn the switch on in our life, we will merely be existing and just moving about. Work and moving about are two different things. When one works, he has a purpose or meaning in what he is doing; so he puts his life in it. Therefore, every work is an accomplishment, a fulfillment, and it is a joy. However, on the contrary, if one works without a purpose or willingness, his work is not work. It is lifeless and it amounts to just moving about.

A wire with current is called a live wire. Many so-called poems are mere words which are beautifully arranged, but some true poems have life in them. They are living and touch the hearts of people. This is true in calligraphy, paintings, and also in meetings and gatherings. Some meetings are said to be dead because there is no interesting thing and no vital concern about life.

When one falls in love, life takes on a new meaning. His whole life becomes alive; in fact, the whole world becomes alive. It is the same when one discovers himself, that is to say, when he finds what he really wants to do or discovers something for which he wants to dedicate his life. Then his life has some meaning and becomes very much alive.

When we start to see light, the whole world becomes bright and the light shines upon us. Each day is not mere passing of another day, but is significant and meaningful, a most worthy and reverent day. It is a day of accomplishment and thankfulness.

GAUTAMA BUDDHA

It was about 2500 years ago that Siddhartha Gautama was born as the only son of the famous King Suddhodana of Kapilavastu, which was in the northern part of India. Siddhartha's mother was the beautiful Queen Maya. He was a boy like any boy, full of ambition and energy. Being the Crown Prince, he received the best education of his time. He was the best horseback rider and a fine wrestler and archer, as well as a mental genius. As he grew older, he became interested in learning the cause of all of life's sufferings. He became contemplative, lost interest in sports and politics, and despite his father's request that he be the next king, he left his father's beautiful palace and became a truth seeker. He was then 29.

For the next six years he wandered through the country seeking teachers and teachings by which he could solve the many problems of life. First he went to the Brahmins and tried their philosophy in solving human problems. Then he studied in a group of ascetics, undertaking their severe, ascetic life. And so he went on for six years trying every school of religion and philosophy but in vain. None of the schools gave him a satisfactory answer.

One day, after cleansing himself in the waters of the Nairanjana, he sat under a pippal tree and meditated, and there, after years of observation and experience, he at last found the truth, attained enlightenment, and called himself Buddha. He was then 35. Until then, Prince Siddhartha had not been Buddha.

"Buddha" is a Sanskrit term meaning "Enlightened One." Buddha was not a deity, not any kind of god, nor was he a man of revelation as in many other religions. Buddha was a man who found the truth and lived the truth.

Buddha lived to 80 years of age, and so, for 45 years, he taught the way of life that he found himself. He was a practical, realistic philosopher, psychologist and spiritual leader. He was the first to deny the caste system, saying that a man should be judged by his quality, not by his birth. Thus, against the strong conformity of his time, he was brave enough to denounce the entrenched caste system of India. He was against the complex religious rituals of his day; he did away with anthropomorphic concepts, and he did not believe in the dualistic idea of an independent self or soul as such, as a separate entity. He explained that all things are related to each other through the Law of causation.

Buddha, after his enlightenment, gave his first sermon at the Deer Park on the outskirts of the city of Benares. The contents of the first sermon were the famous Four Noble Truths and Eightfold Path, which are the foundation of the

Buddhist teachings.

Buddha's teaching is not theology nor metaphysics. Buddha did not speculate on that which is unknowable, such as an unknowable beginning or end. There is no beginning and no end in eternity. He did not conceptualize eternity. Eternity is now. The present moment includes the eternal past and the eternal future. It is the eternal-present. Buddha was interested in the present. There are many urgent and pressing problems right here and now in our life. Solving the present problems also solves those past and future. Buddha's teachings start from his own observations and experiences in life in this world. The Four Noble Truths are:

(1) The recognition of suffering. We do not have to recognize it—we have it. We have much suffering, misery, and trouble in our life. That life involves suffering is a fact, and just this statement of fact—that all beings are subject to suffering—was Buddha's first statement of the Four Noble Truths. It was not theorizing or speculating but the facts of life, or existence.

(2) The cause of suffering. There are no miracles in Buddhism; suffering has definite causes. Buddha was like a physician who diagnoses a patient and finds the cause of his disease. That is why he was often called the physician of life. The cause of suffering is ignorance.

(3) The overcoming or transcending of the causes of suffering. Ignorance, the cause of suffering, must and can be overcome or transcended. Therefore, Buddhism is the way of enlightenment.

(4) The way to overcome the cause of suffering. The way is the Eightfold Path.

The Eightfold Path is symbolized in the wheel of law or wheel of life, which is the international symbol of Buddhism. The eight spokes of the wheel represent the eight ways of life or law which are in motion. The wheel symbolizes the motion. Life is dynamic and ever in motion. The eight spokes spread out from the hub, which symbolizes truth, and the spokes are encompassed by the tire or rim, which represents wisdom and compassion. The Eightfold Path comprises: right understanding, right thinking, right speech, right conduct, right effort, right occupation, right mindfulness, and right meditation. By living the Eightfold Path, one can overcome the causes of trouble and suffering.

The frequent misunderstandings and lack of understanding in private or domestic and in social and international life show how much we need right understanding in our life. We need right understanding about things, events, and relationships, as well as about life itself, to overcome the many troubles caused by ignorance.

The meaning of this "right," as used throughout the Eightfold Path, is very important. It is not right compared with wrong. It is right in the absolute sense and not in a moral and relative sense. There is only the right. The right is the transcended right which is over and beyond the duality of right and wrong. Right or truth changes according to different situations and conditions and times. There is no unchanging, permanent, static truth or right. Therefore, the right means in an absolute and religious sense and not in a moral or ethical sense.

Right occupation means work to which one can put one's whole life. It is a life work. Many people think of work as a means for "making a living." They choose a job because of pay, prestige, or because it is easy. But right occupation means life itself. Every work is noble and right if it is one's life's work. The life of dedication is the right occupation, and the occupation means the life of dedication. Wrong occupation brings continuous troubles and sufferings to oneself and others. Right occupation is very important in right living.

Buddha understands the world in which we live as continuous change. Everything changes; nothing is permanent. All material things, ideas, ideals, character and personality, morals, cultures, economic conditions, political situations, and all that exist are in constant change. Because of this continuous changing of all things, we are constantly having to meet new situations, and this creates many problems and, frequently, sufferings. Since we are always confronted with problems, the Buddhist view of life as always being subject to suffering is so true.

Ignorance is the cause of all troubles and sufferings. Ignorance about oneself is the greatest ignorance. The Buddha's first teaching in the search of the way was first to know yourself. Socrates devoted his whole life to "know thyself," and Buddha taught the same way. One must know what he is before he can do anything to attain peace, happiness, or freedom. Many people think they know what they are, but we have to remember that yesterday's "I" is not today's "I" or the "I" of tomorrow. We are continuously living new life. There is no self as such that does not change. This is the doctrine of "non-self" or no-self. What "I am" is the sum total of other things and people. There is no unchanging and eternal self or soul as such. This does not mean the denial of individuality. Buddha emphatically emphasized the uniqueness and importance of an individual. "Be yourself" is the important teaching in Buddhism. However, one should not cling to a concept of an unchanging self.

All of Buddha's teachings point to the immediacy, spontaneity, non-attachment, non-duality, and oneness in life. Though Buddha was born 2500 years ago in India, his life is ever new and fresh in me here today in America. Only when I see myself truly, Gautama Buddha is present in me. His life is my life; my life is everyone's life. All life is one. That is the life of Gautama Buddha.

THOUGHTS FOR THE NEW YEAR

"Shinnen akemashite omedeto." This is "A Happy New Year" greeting in Japanese. It means, literally, congratulations that a new year has "opened up."

Some people say that sending New Year greeting cards is a mere formality. But it is not a formality to me. It is a very important and opportune time to greet many friends. It is a very happy time for me. I have neglected many friends through the year, not writing or calling, and I would like to visit them at least once at the new year to say hello or to send greetings to let friends know that we are all well.

Many people send me a greeting card. Each card brings a happy greeting and is such a joy to receive. Some say that they have moved and others report an addition to the family or that they have lost dear ones. I have sent a little over thousand cards this year. My daughter helped me, but with every one I took care as if I were visiting my friends personally. My thought was with them. It is a wonderful season and it is a very happy time to send greeting cards.

New Year comes only to those who welcome it. After all, it is we who make a new year. It is in the culture; it is in our minds. There are different New Years such as the Chinese New Year and the Jewish New Year, according to their traditions. Unless we make it, the new year is not there. I do not think that there is a new year in a dog's life. So we should not take the New Year for granted as a mere formality. We have to make it a new year, and we should make it an important thing.

I feel so much about warm-heart nowadays. There were times I thought so much of justice, and at other times, of reason and rationality, and sometimes I thought of money and health. These things are very important, there is no question of that. But nowadays I feel a deep longing for warmth of life. My two New Year poems this year are:

> *Holding a warm heart,*
> *Together with people,*
> *I will move forward;*
> *Oh, this good year.*
>
> * *
>
> *
>
> *More than money, more than reason,*
> *More than anything else,*
> *How I long for a warm heart of man.*

It is the warmth that makes life grow. The late Dr. Kuki once said that he became a Buddhist because Buddhist life is warm. As I read the accounts and teachings of Gautama

Buddha, I saw that more people became his disciples because of his profound understanding and warmth than because of convincing reason or rationality. That is why there are no missionaries propagating Buddhism. The all-important thing is that each Buddhist live his good Buddhist life.

Another thought for the New Year is the way of "let it go" or non-attachment. We cling too much to many things. We create troubles, tensions, and many problems because we are so possessive and clinging. We have to learn the doctrine of non-attachment and "let it go." "Let it go" does not mean carelessness or neglect, just as non-attachment is not indifference or aloofness. It is simply freedom from clinging and possessiveness.

When you do something, do it with all your might. Put your life into it. But do not possess or be possessed by it. Do not cling to it. When it is finished, let it go.

Many mothers kill their only son because of clinging or possessive love. One must let him go when he is grown, as cubs are pushed off by the mother lion. Lovers should love, but should not possess; when love becomes possession, it spoils. Money is a wonderful thing and a very important thing in modern life, but when one clings to it, he becomes a miser, and when one is possessed by money, there is no life. If one clings to opposition, that becomes anger. If one clings to well-being, that becomes greed.

It is so easy to cling to words and actions that others have said and done in the past, and thus we create problems. We cling to the past and neglect the present. The world and life are continually changing, so instead of clinging to the past, we have to live a fresh new life each day. Nor should one cling to the future and neglect the present, because the future is unknown and yet to come. We should live the best in the present.

In the last analysis, all things in this world and life come and go as they will. Let the Way take the ways and let go your own clinging. This is the greatest release. Even to life we should not cling, but let it go, and we are able to live freely. Many deaths were transcended by letting go.

These are my thoughts for the New Year.

STORY OF A CRUTCH

When I visited a Nisei family some time ago, I was asked about Buddhism and the following conversation took place.

"Reverend, my parents were Buddhists, but I haven't learned Buddhism. I went to a Christian church because it was in our neighborhood. As I matured, I wanted to learn about Buddhism, which my parents lived. Will you tell me what Buddhism is, or some of its basic teachings?"

Yes, I will tell you briefly. Buddhism is a religion of enlightenment and a way of life. It is not a religion of belief. Therefore, there is no dogma to believe and no creed to follow. Buddhism teaches to see and understand life and things correctly as they are, and teaches right living.

Everyone, regardless of his status and conditions—whether rich or poor, healthy or ill, man or woman, young or old, black or white—has his own problems. No man is free from suffering. Even the very fortunate have some kind of trouble. It was to meet the problems of human life that the different religions came into being. The purpose of all religions is to solve human problems.

Some people, instead of facing and solving their problems, try to escape from them but only create more problems that way. Some people, although they have problems, simply ignore them as if they did not exist; such people live a double life and are always gloomy in their internal life. Some people drink in order to forget their problems, some people move away, and in extreme cases some commit suicide.

Other people think that man is weak, and believe that there is a superhuman and supernatural being who can help him. These people believe that there is a supreme being who is a creator, sustainer, protector, and judge, and who is almighty. They, therefore, pray to this being for the cure of human troubles; they pray to him, worship and glorify him, and ask his mercy.

Buddhism is altogether different from these two attitudes. It teaches a self-responsible way of life. It teaches the truth or facts of life and the world in order that we see and understand life as it is and things as they are. Life is very hard sometimes. There are much suffering and many problems, but we should neither try to ignore or escape them, nor should we depend on an external agent for their solution. We have to accept these problems ourselves, accept them dynamically. For this, we need profound understanding and courage.

"But, Reverend, don't you think we need a crutch since man is weak?"

Yes, maybe a crutch is necessary for some people. But don't you think we want to see a man who can walk by himself without a crutch? Isn't it a pity to see a man walk with a crutch his whole life? We like to see everyone able to stand up and walk freely as an independent man. I think this attitude shows a true kindness and love to others.

Buddhism teaches a man to be able to stand up by himself and walk by himself. The teachings make a man independent and free. All the teachings are like a pointing finger that points the way. But we have to walk; no one walks for us.

"But, in Buddhism, don't people recite Nembutsu or Namu Amida Butsu in order to be saved? Is it not a prayer? Don't Buddhists pray or ask for mercy to Buddha?"

Oh, no. Buddha is not a god of any kind. Buddha is a man who has attained enlightenment. He is the teacher who wants us to become, like himself, free, independent, and enlightened. Nembutsu is an expression of gratitude. Nembutsu is a voice that is manifested when the eternal or true life is realized in the individual's life. It is an inner voice of man when the finite and infinite are unified or when subject and object become one. It is a great feeling of gratitude when the ego self disappears and completely becomes one with others.

When we are truly able to see and understand life, its reality, its value and beauty as well as its troubles, we are able to accept life dynamically and walk its path with appreciation and gratitude. This way of life is Buddhism.

SELFLESSNESS

Please keep in mind that this was written in the middle of the last century, and there were cultural attitudes in place that have since changed. Bright Dawn—and Rev. Kubose's dharma heirs, more generally—don't discriminate or otherwise make distinctions based on gender. --ED

The self is very much emphasized in modern life. Self is very important because it is a unit of our social structure and therefore the base of all things. So we talk of self-education, self-development, self-service, and so on.

However, when we stop and think what self is, we see a different picture of self. There is no self, really, without the other. Self is a relative thing, and real self is in the selflessness state.

What is the self? Walt Whitman once said that modern people think that self is something that lies between one's shoes and one's hat. That is far from the truth. Buddha said, "The essence of all things is selfless." What we usually think of as the self is very temporal and an illusion. Most people think "I" is the most important thing: "I believe this," "I did that," "I have the right," etc. But "I" is the sum total of all other people and things.

My body is given me by my parents; all the foods that I eat to maintain my growth and existence are produced and provided by others; all the clothing that I wear to protect me are products of other people; my shelter and all other belongings are not of my own making. The languages I speak, I have learned. The way I think, I have learned. My parents, teachers, and all other people taught me. Thus, all that I am is the sum total of others. There is no "I" as such apart from others.

Buddha did not consider the I or self to be an eternal, independent, categorical entity, as is the ātman or soul of Hinduism or Christianity. Life is a continuous becoming. It continuously changes. "I" has many states, always changing. I am father because of children; I am husband because of wife; I am teacher because of students; I am old because I am compared with young. It is all relative existence.

The essence or nature of life is self-less. Only when one is in selflessness is there real peace, beauty, and happiness. In selflessness is the true self. When a mother does things for her child, she does everything for the child without reservation. Even when her life is in danger, she does for her child. We say the mother "sacrifices" for her child, but it is not sacrifice. It is really a fulfillment of her life, because mother and child are one. A person may be frail but become a strong parent, because a mother becomes selfless when she has a child.

When a person is in true love, he will give his life, because a true lover becomes so selfless. His happiness is her happiness and his suffering is her suffering. When lovers meet together as one, there is great beauty, happiness, and peace. It is a great joy to give one's life for someone whom one truly loves or respects. And it is possible because selflessness has such power. Parents should not underestimate the power of love; their fragile, gentle daughter has the power to turn the world upside down when she is in love.

Work that one likes is another area where the truth of selflessness can be observed. The person working forgets himself in his work, forgets the time, his meals, and other things. He and his work are one. He puts his whole life into it. It is a joy for him to work. All dedicated people are selfless in their work. A true religious leader selflessly dedicates his life, because he and people are one. A scientist gives his life for science because he and science are one. Selflessness has such beauty, and is so strong.

In archery or in playing golf, if one is selfish or self-conscious, he cannot do his best. After being well-disciplined or practiced in the sport, if one is selfless in its purpose, his effortless effort can accomplish far greater results than conscious effort and purposive determination.

Flowers bloom selflessly, wind blows selflessly, water flows selflessly, and children are selfless in their words and acts. That is why they are beautiful.

Buddha taught selflessness as one of his three basic teachings. It is our mistaken ego selfishness that causes all human troubles and sufferings. We do not realize that we are literally able to live and enjoy life only because of other people and things. If one really understands this truth, he cannot help but become humble and appreciate others. Buddhism is the way of selflessness.

THE MIND'S EYE

If we have the things we want, if we are satisfied by the life we are living, then we do not need enlightenment; we do not need any philosophy or religion. If all goes well with you, you do not need any philosophy or religion. If all goes well with you, you do not need enlightenment. We need enlightenment or philosophy or religion because we are not satisfied with what we have or with our life today.

Buddha said we are subject to suffering. He proclaimed the universality of suffering. No matter who we are—healthy or weak, young or old, beautiful or ugly—all of us are subject to suffering. Naturally, we would like to transcend our troubles; we would like to solve the problems. But how? And many times we do not know how. Therefore, enlightenment is very important—more than important, it is a necessity of life.

Enlightenment is a new point of view in our life and in the world, finding a new angle to see things. D. T. Suzuki said that enlightenment or satori is the opening of the mind's eye. Our mind, neither stale nor cold, will blossom forth, because of the beautiful things inside itself, full of admiration, inspiration, and enjoyment. Suzuki said that satori is removing of the bar. Something bothers us, something stops us; there is a bar in our mind. Satori is the taking off of this bar so we can become free. Satori is brightening up of the mind's work.

In neurosis, there is something in the mind that the person cannot pass over; he cannot solve his problems; he is unable to control his own mind. The neurotic mind is all covered up and tightened. There may be more than one bar to hinder his free activity. Our inner essence wishes to be free and can be free, but some external things stop the freedom of our mind. To have satori or to enlighten oneself is to free oneself from external bondage.

Buddha proclaimed that all of us have Buddha nature, Buddhahood—not only in man, but in all beings and in all things, there is Buddha nature. Everyone is free, nothing hinders, if you awaken to that true essence of man, the true nature of man. To this end, Buddha teaches meditation, contemplation. But enlightenment is not mere contemplation or mental tranquilization in the usual sense. In Buddhist meditation or contemplation, a person becomes quiet so as to be able to see things as they are.

Satori or enlightenment is a very dynamic thing, not mere quietude. Satori gives a person a turning point in his mental activities. Suzuki said that satori is the turning of the mental hinges. This turning of mental hinges opens the door to other worlds.

Our minds, our mental activities, are usually based on

dualistic concepts: I and he; I and the world; true and false. This world of ours is full of contradictions, and these contradictions cannot be solved. When contradictions cannot be solved, one becomes frustrated, hysterical, neurotic, and may finally end in a nervous breakdown. But in satori, contradictions become non-contradictions.

Contradictions cannot be solved as such. For example, east is east; west is west. East cannot at the same time be west. But in enlightenment, east can at the same time be west. You and I are different, but, at the same time, you and I are one. In Buddhism, in the content of enlightenment, two different things are one. Two beings are different and identical at the same time.

There is an old Zen story: In the yard of a Zen temple, near the front gate, grew an age-old crooked pine tree. The Master of that temple put out a sign which said, "If anyone sees this pine tree straight, I will give him my temple." The tree was so crooked by years of growth that many passersby thought, "How interesting! But how can one see that pine tree straight? It is impossible."

As you know, we think of a straight line and a crooked line as two different lines; a straight tree and a bent, crooked tree as two different things. We cannot see the crooked tree as a straight tree. That is the problem. And so the Zen master said that, to anyone who saw this crooked tree as a straight tree, he would give his temple. All tried to solve this problem, but no one was able to give the master a satisfactory answer. Finally, the master explained that to see that crooked tree as straight is to see that *crooked tree as crooked.*

That is very important. To see the crooked tree as crooked is to see that tree straight. Accepting it as it is; that is straight. You cannot make the tree straight; it would break.

It is similar to meeting an insane person on the sidewalk who happens to spit at you. Not knowing he is insane, you become very angry; you are bewildered, insulted. A little farther down the street you learn that this person is insane. Now that you see him as he is, you are no longer bewildered and hurt. If you had understood that man as being insane, you would not have been insulted by what he did. You would have paid no attention, and not become angry. You have to see a person as he is.

This happens between husband and wife. One expects certain things, a certain way, from the other, but the other person acts according to his own way, not according to these expectations. So one is upset and angry. Similarly, when we are dealing with children, we have to understand children as they are. We want to see things the way we want to; that is the difficulty. If you see things as they are, much can be solved without getting angry or insulted. It is like seeing that crooked pine tree in the temple yard just as it is.

Buddha taught the seeing of the true nature of yourself as well as of all other things. But we often live by external regulations, external forces, external fashions. Take some part of your own life: How much are you living by your own inner life and how much are you forced by some outside thing?

When you completely surrender and live by outside forces, there are no problems. But when you find contradictions—when there is something you want to do from within and the outside forces hinder that inner urge, then you have a conflict; you have a problem. All neurosis is this conflict: something of your own that you want to unfold and something that stops this unfolding. Enlightenment unbinds this knot; it is the enlightenment of the totality of your own life.

We all have experienced partial enlightenment. For example, when we have been pondering and pondering on a problem in mathematics, and suddenly, "Eureka!" we find the way to solve it. It is like a flash of light. It brightens. We have a new point of view to solve the problem. This is a kind of enlightenment. In many things, in all scientific discoveries, there is some kind of enlightenment. But this enlightenment is partial, and everyone has this kind of experience. Whether physical or mental or spiritual, we all have such enlightening experiences in many ways.

Buddhist enlightenment does not concern one particular thing but the fundamental source of life; the whole life is enlightened, and the perspective of life is changed. A new world opens for the person.

There are many example of this total enlightenment or satori in Zen stories. For instance, Joshu, a famous Zen monk, studied very hard at the Zen Temple under his master, but he was unable to enlighten himself, and he often questioned the master in a most complicated and agonized way. One day, after such questions, the master merely responded by asking, "Did you eat breakfast?" "Yes, I did," answered Joshu. "Then did you wash the dishes?" Joshu was at once enlightened.

Another story is that of Tokuzan. Tokuzan was meditating in the temple one twilight, and, as it was getting dark, he went outside to meditate where the moon was shining and it was serene and beautiful. His master came by and said, "Oh, you are meditating here. Why don't you come inside the temple?" "It is too dark inside," answered Tokuzan. "Well, I will give you a light. Why don't you come in," said the master. So Tokuzan went inside, where the master lit a candle and told Tokuzan to place the candle on the table and then meditate. Tokuzan thanked him and, just as the master was handing the lit candle to Tokuzan, he blew it out, plunging the room back into darkness. Tokulzan was immediately enlightened, he attained satori. How? That is up to you; the master merely points the way.

Zen stories are very difficult. As it is said, we learn the hard way. For instance, when I was living in Oakland, I had a friend, Mr. Tagara, who was a very capable man, a very learned person, a community leader. He was a poet, a leading poet, and was able to compose beautiful haiku and waka. He was an able speaker and the whole community looked up to him for leadership and admired him. He and his wife had three children, his business was very good, and they bought a house in Berkeley.

Everyone thought that Mrs. Tagara must be the most fortunate wife to have such an able and good husband. But

Mrs. Tagara was not happy. She was also sickly, somewhat neurotic. Why was she not happy despite everyone's guess? Mr. Tagara was a very able man. He was not only very intelligent and a community leader, he was even a very good cook. If she knew one thing, he knew two or three. How could even a very intelligent wife match such a husband? She had done her best to make him happy, but he was never satisfied. "You are clumsy; you could do better," he would say. So through all their marriage, the wife suffered from feelings of inferiority.

One summer, Mr. Tagara unfortunately had eye trouble. All that summer he went to the doctor, but his eyes became worse and worse. That fall, he finally lost his eyesight. He became blind. You can imagine what a change this was to such a man. He had been so able in every way, but now he could not read a newspaper or go for a walk or even go to the bathroom without asking his wife or daughter to take him. Mr. Tagara had never bowed his head before. Now he had to beg, to ask everything from other people.

Being such an able man, Mr. Tagara had never had good friends. He felt that all his friends were inferior, and he could not appreciate their friendship. He had a very close friend called Yamada, who often came to visit him. But Mr. Tagara would say, "Oh, that Yamada comes again and talks nonsense. I wish he wouldn't come, as I have many books to read." He never appreciated Yamada's visits because Yamada never talked on the same level as Mr. Tagara. Mr. Tagara wanted to read books rather than have mediocre friends come to waste his time.

But when he became blind, he could not read a book. When he heard footsteps on the front porch: "Oh, it is Yamada. I am glad he is coming." And before Yamada could knock on the door, Mr. Tagara would call, "Is that Yamada?" "Yes," Yamada would answer. "I'm so glad you came. What's the news in the world?" Mr. Tagara would exclaim.

Yamada had not changed, but Mr. Tagara had changed. A 180 degree turn.

One day, Tagara called his wife, Yoshiko-san, "Yoshiko, come here." Yoshiko-san thought that she was to be scolded again, so she rather hesitated. "Do you want something?" she asked. "Sit here," her husband said. She sat down. "Sit closer. Sit next to me." Yoshiko-san did not understand why he wanted her to sit close to him. Tagara took Yoshiko-san's hand and all of a sudden there were tears in his eyes.

"Yoshiko," he said, "I realize for the first time what you have suffered for so many years. We have been married almost 20 years. I was so stubborn; I had such a superiority complex. All your years of ill health were caused by my stubbornness. For the first time I understand real kindness, the many services you did for me which I never appreciated before." Both of them hugged each other and cried, a cry of joy. It was the first time the two of them understood each other.

Since then, new life came into their home, her health started to improve, and he became very humble, yet he did not lose his dignity and superior quality. Friends meeting him on the street would say, "Tagara-san, I am sorry you have lost your vision." "Oh," he would answer, "don't say you're sorry. You should congratulate me on the loss of my eyesight." Everyone was dumbfounded when he said this. "I have lost my physical eye, but I have found my mind's eye. Now I am able to understand what love is. For the first time I notice what friendship is, what sympathy is. You know, a stubborn guy like me, unless my eyes are crushed, is unable to find this new world. I wish you would congratulate me that I lost my vision but found my mental eye."

Mr. Tagara was a completely changed man. He was enlightened. He was enlightened to a completely new world. He had transcended his small petty individualism and was able to see and join in a greater world and oneness of all life. He found himself in a world of love, of friendship. This kind of experience is called enlightenment.

Buddha's enlightenment was comprehensive in all respects. But we too are able to understand and taste and open our new point of view. Enlightenment was not just Gautama Buddha's, but you too, individually, must find this new perspective of life, this new point of view in your life and in all things. That is satori. It must be yours and can be yours. No one can give it to you. You have to find it yourself. Yes, it is difficult, but it is yours, and there it is. But, in fact, you do not look for satori because you are already in it. You are in that enlightenment; just open your mind and there you will find new light, new perspective.

HONESTY

Honesty is one of the most important qualities of man's integrity and every religion teaches us to be honest, as in the Ten Commandments "Thou shalt not lie," and in the Buddhist Five Precepts "Do not speak a word which is not true." It is the fundamental principle of ethical law and it is said "Honesty is the best policy."

I was asked the other day about honesty, especially in Buddhism. Therefore, I should like to write an essay on honesty and share the teaching.

Honesty, in general, is applied in the relationship between people. That is to say, one should be honest to his parents and friends. One is said to be an honest man because he does not tell a lie to people and society. One is punished by law for being dishonest. Therefore, honesty is a very important factor in social education. We are taught to be honest from the time we are able to speak and understand, and it is the foundation of social life.

Religiously, honesty is implied in one's own life. It is more important to be honest to oneself than honest to others. Honesty is quite subjective in religion as compared with the objective sense in ethics. There are many people who tell lies to themselves and get sick later by internal disturbances. It is easy to tell lies to others but one can not cheat himself. In order to smooth out an incident or affair, one tells lies to get away. Many people put up a false front—telling lies—to gain money, power or prestige. One can deceive others easily but he cannot fool himself. He knows that he is not honest to himself. Dishonesty to oneself is the cause of disturbances in one's inner life, and it is the cause of unhappiness and neurosis.

There are many smooth talkers and many people who put up a false front and live double lives, but I would rather be cheated and be happy, and be poor by being honest, rather than cheat others for gain. There is untold peace and gladness in being honest to myself. Indeed, honesty is the problem concerning oneself and not in relation to others.

RIGHT UNDERSTANDING

Right understanding is the first step of the Noble Eightfold Path and it is the most important one. We are long trained and habituated to understand things dualistically and it is so hard to transcend the dualistic concept, to understand things in totality or in oneness. Right understanding is the understanding of things as they are without any comparison. It is a way of viewing things as unique totality.

We judge things in comparison and say this is good or bad, right or wrong, beautiful or ugly. We judge things according to our taste and convenience. And again we judge things by our own standard and say that one is civilized or uncivilized or barbarian. To compare and judge things by dividing is the characteristic of the Western World, which is based on the dualistic concept of creator and created, God and man, reward and punishment, right and wrong, conqueror and conquered, etc. Perhaps this is a development of the Judeo-Christian concept of dualism of creator and created.

According to this way of thinking and understanding,

everything must be judged as right or wrong, this or that. It is a philosophy of "either-or" and a culture of morality. In this philosophy everything is a conflict and competition. Therefore, winning is very important. Unless you win, you must lose. In such a world, co-existence or becoming one is very difficult. Therefore, if wife is right, then husband is wrong. It must be democracy or else communism. One must be a friend or else an enemy. If one believes a certain faith, then he tries to convert others because he thinks that his is the best and the others are wrong or inferior. The "I am right and he is wrong" idea makes one aggressive and accusatory, and become self-praise and conceit. On the other hand, one becomes pessimistic and has a defeated attitude by saying "they are rich but I am poor," or "she is beautiful but I am not." In such a world there are always competition, conflict, fear, and all kinds of complexes.

Right understanding is not such comparison. It goes beyond relative values. It transcends dualistic comparison. Right understanding means to recognize the uniqueness of each, to understand things as they are. In Buddhism Nyorai (Tathagata) is used as a title like the word, Buddha; for instance, Amida-Nyorai, Shaka-Nyorai, Yakushi-Nyorai, Dainichi-Nyorai. Nyorai means thus come, or come as it is, or be as it is. There is a well-known quotation, "Flowers are red and leaves are green." It is just so. In the Amida Sutra it describes that "red color has red light, white color has white light." Capitalism, communism and democracy have their places according to time, place and conditions. We possess all those elements in us and we can not be purely democratic or communistic. It is not communism or democracy that is bad, but it is the selfishness and the spirit of conquering others that is bad.

As long as there is wrong as compared with right, that right is not the right. The right is beyond right and wrong. The good is beyond good and bad. The true beauty transcends the comparative beauty and uglyness. Understand a child as a child; understand an adult as she is or as he is. Then many problems can be solved. A piano is a piano, a violin a violin, a flute a flute, a drum a drum. All are unique and independent, but when they are played together, a symphony is created. Leaves are leaves and they are green and flowers are flowers and they are red. So, you are you and you ought to be the best of you. You need not compare yourself with the next person. Why do you compete and try to win? Why are you afraid to be defeated? No one can defeat you. You can not be defeated because you are you.

HEALTHFUL OUTLOOK TOWARD LIFE AND DEATH

Life becomes very different according to one's view of it. For example, one's outlook or attitude toward life and death can make one either easily upset and gloomy or can make one's life harmonious, peaceful and bright.

I should like to examine a healthful outlook toward life and death, because different religion, cultures and races have different perspectives on life, death, nature, morality, politics, etc.

Our American culture emphasizes youth, growth, progress, success; and it does not consider old age and death as part of birth and growth. Old age is considered ugly and as something to struggle against, and inevitable death is hated and feared. But life includes both life and death, and they cannot be separated. Life is not only youth or growth; it includes death also. Old age and death are not ugly or hateful; they should be understood as part of growth and maturity. Mature age is beautiful and death is part of nature.

The other day, a traveler from Asia said that American

culture has no philosophy of the aged and death, and that its view of life is therefore shallow. Perhaps this thought was due to the nature of this country, which is young and growing, or perhaps because too much emphasis is put on youth, beauty and growth. However, as in any other country, we here too are born, we mature and we die. Yet our culture is one of such thorough-going dichotomies: we dichotomize life and death, youth and old age, and think that life is good and beautiful, while old age and death are bad and ugly. Therefore, the aged here feel sad and unloved; the young express their dislike of aging; and all fear death. It seems that entire philosophies and religions have developed from the fear of old age and death.

But why do we dichotomize life and death? Buddhism teaches the falsehood of this, for life and death are not opposite but are both phases of one life which are complementary to each other. Just as metabolism in a living organism includes both anabolism and catabolism, so would there be no living life without death as one of its processes. There would be no life without death.

Life and death are neither good nor bad, ugly nor beautiful; they just are as they are—or as you yourself see them. Everyone enjoys the spring buds and soft summer greenness. But are not the dead and golden leaves of autumn also beautiful? It is beautiful to see the golden leaves part from the branches even though there is no wind and dance down to the earth to return to the mother ground. Autumn foliage is more poetic than the summer green. Spring is romantic, but autumn is serene and meditative.

Old age and death are natural processes of life and should be regarded as such. An aged person has dignity and wisdom and should be respected and honored. In traditional Japanese culture, the aged are most loved and respected. Grandparents are more loved than parents by the children.

The aged should live as aged, not competing with the young, and vice versa. To compare and compete is to create problems. The aged yield, the young listen; this is harmony and the law of complementaries, just as heaven and earth, and plus and minus, and Yin and Yang harmonize and become one. Life is one; this is the beauty in life. Unity in diversity; this is the beauty in nature.

Our life has become too utilitarian in this machine culture, in which anything that does not produce is considered useless and must be thrown away. The aged are useless because they no longer produce, so they are ignored or treated with contempt. It seems, with our pragmatic philosophy and utilitarian culture, that our life has become a producing machine and has lost its beauty and warmth.

Life is noble; so death is noble. It is a completion and fulfillment of one's life. It is better to die in nobleness than to live in dishonesty and disgrace. How to die nobly and peacefully as well as live nobly and peacefully is religion. When one lives each eternal moment fully and honestly, he can die most nobly and peacefully. There is an old saying in Japan that it is better to die as a precious jewel breaks than to exist as a broken brick.

We live by death. Flower petals scatter, but leave their fragrances; man dies but leaves his name. Quảng Đức, the South Vietnamese monk, lived by dying. He dedicated and fulfilled his life by his death. His death was not suicide nor sacrifice. It was a most sincere and brave appeal to his own government to correct the wrong suppression of Buddhists. An old Chinese proverb says that death is lighter than a piece of fur from a cow. Patrick Henry shouted, "Give me liberty or give me death!" and Daisuke Itagaki said, "Though Itagaki die, liberty will not die." These statements indicate that death was lighter for these men than giving up the principle for which they lived.

Death is not much of a problem, but how to live is an important problem. "The longer he lives, the more disgrace there is"—if we are speaking of a dishonest man. If one understands the principle of life, then death is no problem. Life and death are one and inseparable. We die but we do not die. We live beyond life and death. We must fully live this eternal today.

BEYOND THE RELATIVE WORLD

We are living in the relative world, that is to say, we are related to each other. Indeed, we are interrelated and interdependent. No one is able to live without other people and things. In fact, all are one. This relativeness, however, should not be opposed to each other. Whenever relativeness becomes in opposition or becomes either extreme dependency or aggressiveness, it creates troubles and sufferings.

We have tendencies to oppose others, to blame others, and this is the cause of sufferings in human relations. There was a couple who had three children. The husband loved wine and gambling. The wife, a very intelligent woman, tried very hard to correct him, but he became worse and many evenings he did not come home. The wife's rage was so great that she could not sleep. She lost her appetite and her health began to fail. It was only natural for her to become angry and disgusted with life. Many of her friends comforted and advised her. Two of them told her that, of course, her husband is wrong in his behavior, but for him to become as he is, she has some responsibility. He is bad, true, but she is also bad, so she should look into herself, too. She did not take this advice, because she believed that she did not do anything wrong.

I was asked to talk to her and one evening she came to me. After I heard her whole story, I agreed with everything she told me. She was quite pleased and happy. She was taken aback, however, when I told her that I would not say that her husband and she were both at fault, but that she was solely responsible for her sufferings. Naturally, she asked forcibly, why this was so. In the relative world, I told her, where things are compared, her husband is wrong and she is right. But for her to condemn him, fight with him, become angry with him, become disgusted with life, pity herself and become ill and neglect her children; in that she is at fault. Her good and right become bad, and she is responsible for her sufferings and miseries. She understood and agreed with me; and then, I told her that there is a world where she does not have to suffer, there is a way to free herself and I knew she could do it. She asked how she could do this and overcome her sufferings. She must go beyond the relative world, I answered; this means to go beyond comparison and oppositions. She must establish her own life, which will not be suppressed or victimized by others. She understood and started to live her own life without being bothered by her husband's wrong life. She beautifully overcame the situation and started a new life.

One of my friends told about his recent experience of being splashed with water from a third floor window as he walked by. He was not the only one as many other passers-by had this experience. He thought that a teenager was doing this and was quite concerned as well as annoyed. He was very watchful for some time. One day he saw who was doing it, and much to his surprise he saw, not a teenager, but a man! And with him were two children. A father and his children were enjoying themselves by pouring water on people. When he discovered this fact, he could not say a word. His annoyance was gone and he thought, "Oh, this foolish man is wasting his time and his life by doing such a thing." Suddenly, however, he asked himself, "What about me? I am doing the same thing. I was annoyed by someone who did not know any better and I am wasting my time and my life by becoming annoyed." His thoughts changed to compassion; the opposition disappeared and he and the man became one.

We are living in a culture of dichotomy and we objectify others as if they are in opposition to us. As soon as we realize this, we should also realize that what is in opposition is our own shadow. When we see others in us or ourselves in others, we overcome opposition and the relative world and become one. In recognizing others as such in the highest sense, there is respect for others as well as for ourselves. Only when we respect ourselves in the true sense of the word, can we truly respect others.

BUDDHISM, ZEN AND NEMBUTSU

Buddhism is a way of life as compared with a religion of believing. Buddhism is self-fulfillment, self-development, a creative life. It is a way of life. It is philosophy, psychology, and religion—not just believing, but immediate and direct. Everything in life is religion—is the Buddhist way. Especially in Zen, where they say that getting up in the morning, brushing your teeth, washing your face—all this is religion.

Each day, every moment of life, is a religion in itself. How to live, how to find yourself in the multiplicity, the complexity of life today is to find the simple pure life which you are seeking. This is what Zen teaches. This is what Buddhism as a whole teaches, a way of life whereby you can find peace, joy, and harmony with your environment. Buddhism teaches that whatever exists is the result of karma and that you are responsible, not somebody else. No external agent is responsible for your happiness or misery.

Zen primarily emphasizes meditation. Shin emphasizes Nembutsu. While these approaches may sound different, they really are not. Both reach to complete liberation, deliverance, and attainment of freedom. Through attachment, men often become the slaves of many things. If one becomes a slave of his own passion, this passion grows in him and becomes a misery to himself and others. The Buddhist way of life is the liberation, the deliverance which unties the entangled knots of human troubles. Regardless of which text is used in the various schools of Buddhism, all teach this way of life to come to enlightenment, to deliverance. The content of enlightenment is Nirvana. Nirvana is that totality of life where one finds real peace and joy and harmony. Zen is one of the ways to enlightenment and freedom.

"Zen," the Japanese word, is "Ch'an" in Chinese, "Jhana" in the ancient spoken language of India, and "Dhyana" in Sanskrit. Dhyana is meditation, static and dynamic—not just static quietude, but quietude in the amidst of multiplicity. The school of Zen is becoming widely known today in America and Europe. But, in some circles, it is being misunderstood and corrupted. Some of the so-called "beat" generation have seized on certain parts of Zen without understanding the rest: they just took the "beat" part of Zen. So being beat is quite a fad today—the Bohemian style of living, life as a "beat." Of course, our life *is* a kind of beat—just as our heart beats. As our heart is a continuous beat, so is life a beat; it is not a static thing but a beat. But this beat is not a haphazard thing. It has universal rhythm, is one with the truth. But the beat generation takes just a part of life and says, "I don't care about formality, conformity; I don't care about others, but I live the way I want."

Today, many teenagers are becoming something like this. They have so much energy, they want to do something; but they do not want to conform, they just do the way that they want.

A man is not an independent being, as many teenagers think. A man is a being who is very closely interdependent and interrelated with other beings. No one can live without others. We are an integral part of the whole. So this life is not a selfish, individual, independent beat, but a beat together. Yes, it is the individual's unique beat, but it is also a beat of the entirety, a beat together of the universe. The individual's beat is the same as the beat of others. Of course, everyone has his unique beat, but his beat is one and the same in this universal rhythm. But this universal beat of Zen has been misunderstood and twisted, turned into a fad. True Zen is not a haphazard, egotistical, individual thing. It is uniquely individual, yet it has universality.

A young man from the northern part of China once walked many hundreds of miles to where Bodhidharma was sitting in meditation. This was a very sincere, earnest young man who, when he found Bodhidharma, said, "My name is so-and-so. I have walked many hundreds of miles to seek the teachings. Please teach me what Buddhism is." Bodhidharma did not look up, gave no response. The young man waited in vain all day, but there was no response. So he stayed there that night. The next morning he again went to the master and once more begged for the teachings. He waited all day but with no results. The third day, the same thing—no response. The young man, somewhat restless, wondered how to get Bodhidharma's attention. For three days Bodhidharma had not even looked at him—not one glance. So the young man had to do something—he grabbed his ear lobe and tore it off and threw it at the master and said, "Master, speak." Bodhidharma for the first time thought that this man must be serious, was really asking for the teachings. He looked at the young man and agreed to let him stay with him. This young man, who was willing to put his whole life into what he wanted, later became Bodhidharma's successor.

When we do something, it should not be in a haphazard way; we have to put our whole life into it. That is the Buddhist attitude. When you play basketball, play basketball—not just swing around. A man, whatever he says or does, puts his whole responsibility and life into his every word. Even if his life is in danger, he can risk his life. Such an attitude is the Buddhist way of life.

I remember one mother in Oakland, California, where I used to live. Her only son loved football very much, but she was against his playing football because many boys were getting hurt. But the boy just begged to play. So one day the mother said, "I don't want you to play football because you might get hurt, but, in spite of my wish, if you're going to play football, play. Even if you're going to die, play. Since you're so much for it, give your life for it. Just don't play for play's sake, but play until your death." This boy became one of the most outstanding football players among the Nisei in northern California. This mother was a true Buddhist.

Japanese mothers, when their sons went to war, always

used to say, "Go and die." This "go and die" in Japanese means to risk your life, to give everything you have. They never said, "Go and come back; do a glorious act and come back." When we are called for duty, we carry on in spite of life. The Buddhist way is to put everything in when you do something—not necessarily in war, but in organizational work or in any line of work. Every man has a life to live, a life to fulfill responsible work. One must achieve honorable work so as to be able to put one's whole life into it. This is the way of Zen in Buddhism. Man and his work are one. Man and his world are one just as a young man and his sweetheart are one. When people love each other, it is mutual. It is one, not one-sided love. A true love is a complete union and oneness. Subject and object become one. When a person loves his work, whatever he does, the work is he and he is the work.

I read a biography of Henry Ford: When he was working on a machine, he worked until 12:00, 1:00, 2:00—many mornings until 3:00—and at 4 o'clock he would go to a coffee shop nearby. When engrossed in his machine, he forgot time, he forgot eating because he was so immersed in his work. There is untold joy in such a way of life. In science and religion, a man who makes a success—I do not really like the word success—is a man who really does his work with life. Take Mahatma Ghandi: what he believed, he lived. Even put into jail, even without eating, Ghandi fulfilled his inner urge to live a life of truth. He lived a life of oneness.

This world of oneness is Nembutsu. Knowing that the so-called pairs of opposites—you and I, society and I, country and

I, parent and child, wife and husband, God and man, creator and created, body and soul, spiritual and material—are all really one, this is Nembutsu. Not one member of any of these pairs can exist without the other. "Husband" is meaningless without "wife." Without a husband, there is no wife. And so on. But in the West, we struggle in the attempt to divide our lives into two. In Buddhism I am the family, the family is I; all these pairs are one. While we are living in complexity, this complexity is not haphazard, but is a definite interdependency, interrelationship. Buddhism teaches the finding of one in the many and the many in one (the diversity in each one of us). This world of oneness is Nirvana; it is Namu Amida-Butsu, and it is Nembutsu.

Nembutsu is the unity of subject and object. Namu Amida-Butsu means that Buddha and I are one, my country and I are one, entire humanity and I are one. When we put our whole life into something, we become one with it. When a man risks his life for mankind, he and mankind are one.

Each one of us, in a small way, is most honorable. Each has a truly sincere purpose to carry out and realize his own potentialities. Therefore, whatever we do, we should do it with all our being. This can be endless to explain. It is not words, not conceptions or ideas, but what we do each day, each moment, with a sense of responsibility and with an attitude of fulfillment. There we find a grateful, joyous life. Such a fulfillment of one's own life means the fulfillment of the world as a whole. This is Nembutsu and this is the essence of Zen.

REALITY OF BROTHERHOOD

When Rev. Kubose wrote this in 1959, he used a word as an ethnic identifier which was considered acceptable at the time, but is now outdated and can be seen as disparaging. The language of living, evolving people itself lives and evolves. During deliberation, we weighed the benefits of recognizing this as a historic document and leaving the essay as written versus changing a few words to fit today's preferred terminology. In the end, we decided to update the term, both to conform with contemporary publishing standards, and in keeping with words we feel Rev. Kubose would have chosen had he written this today. Bright Dawn and Kubose's dharma heirs support efforts to combat systemic racism and to promote diversity, equity and inclusion. We believe the dharma unites all people in Oneness, with no distinction based on age, gender or national/cultural origin. --ED

February 18~24 is National Brotherhood Week. In observance of this week, I believe that each one of us should have a clear understanding of what brotherhood means to himself.

Brotherhood is not merely a word or concept. It is not just

an idea or ideal. And, of course, it is not a slogan, either. Brotherhood is reality. At the Brotherhood Dinner sponsored by the Japanese American Citizens League on February 22, 1959, Dr. Percy Julian, a famous chemist who happens to be Black, spoke emphatically about "Do You Mean What You Say?" Many beautiful speeches are delivered and wonderful essays are written about brotherhood. We talk about equality, justice, and pursuit of happiness. Do we really mean these beautiful words? Brotherhood is not words nor a concept nor something just to talk about. It is life in itself that is lived together in oneness. What I am, my very existence, the very fact of my presence here now is due to my brothers; it is the result of brotherhood. I exist because of the brotherhood. I am the brotherhood. If I should start to analyze all the involvements of brotherhood in which I am, it would take uncountable time.

Life is like a huge mesh net. As the meshes are all interconnected, so are we interrelated and interdependent. We live a mutually cooperative life. Take my coat for instance. It is made of cotton, wool, and silk. The cotton may have been raised by farmers in Texas under the scorching summer heat. The silk may have come from Japan, where the farmers cultivate mulberry trees by which to raise the silkworms. The wool may have come from sheep herders in the high plateaus of Australia. These materials had to be gathered and processed by different field and factory workers, and made into cloth, and still handled by other workers. All the materials had to be transported by ships, trains, and trucks. The store owner made the suit available for me to buy. Just imagine how many people are involved in this suit with which I keep myself warm. Hundreds and thousands of people are involved in every item I use, the food I eat, the place where I live. I am able to exist because of the work and services of these people. My very life is the life of other people and things.

Some people hate those from outside their own ethnic or religious group. Such a person had better not eat or use anything made by them. This, of course, is impossible. Therefore brotherhood is a reality, not just a concept or ideal. Whether you like it or not, there is brotherhood and you are involved in it.

The very fact of life means brotherhood. Brotherhood is not something we must do or should observe. It is a reality that we are. If one realizes this fact of life, this reality and truth of life, he has to live accordingly. The scope of brotherhood is so vast and deep. You cannot escape from it. In Buddhism, this spirit and life of brotherhood extends to animals, plants, and all things as well as men, because all are interrelated, because all life is one. Because all life is one, we respect every life. When we realize the reality of our interdependence, we cannot help becoming harmonious, peaceful, and appreciative of one another and of all things.

NON-DICHOTOMIZATION

Twice annually we observe O-Higan. Astronomically, it is on O-Higan day that the sun rises directly from the east and sets directly in the west. Thus, the length of the day and night are equal. O-Higan also represents a season not too hot, not too cold, thus symbolizing the middle path of Buddhism. Therefore, for many centuries the one week during this time of the equinox(equal night) has been selected as O-Higan week to make an opportunity to gather at temple, listen to lectures, do some social work, observe memorial services to express gratitude, and, in all, to make time for self-reflection—what I am; what is the truth of things. I think that this is the significance of the O-Higan season and services.

"O-Higan" is a Japanese word: "O" is an honorific, and "Higan" means "the other shore." But "Higan" is really an abbreviation of "Tōhigan." "Tō" means "to go across," "Higan" means "the other shore," so "Tōhigan" means "to go across to the other shore." The "Tō" is the more significant part of "Tōhigan." "Higan," unless we are very careful, becomes a concept. But "Tō," go across, going, is not a concept; it is experience, it is living. It is not static. So *go* to the other shore is the important part, and I would like to put the emphasis on "Tō" more than on "Higan" itself. It means to live each day. The destination, goal, end, or "Higan" is eventually reached if we take each step in the perfect way. If the means are perfect, it is only natural to reach the perfect end. So the means are more important than the goal. I should not say more important, as that divides means and ends into two, whereas means *are* ends, ends *are* means. Knowing this, "Higan" becomes perfectly understandable without attaching the verb "Tō." To go *is* the other shore.

Since Higan season is the time for self-reflection, I would like to speak on ego self. It seems that, in what is called the free world, the countries of the West, our civilization and culture are the culmination of the development of the ego self. Our political science, education, economics, and so on, are all pointed toward the development of the individual self. It sounds very logical, very true, to respect the individual, to recognize the dignity of the individual. But we have such a strong inclination to support, develop, expand, and affirm the self. ("Self" may appear to mean the individual without attaching selfishness, while "ego" connotates selfishness; nevertheless, in the essence, self or ego or individual is the same thing, I.) We assert the self, I. I have the right, you have no right to be in my way. Our term of freedom means this development of the self, the ego. We Americans speak of freedom. By declaring freedom, we oppress others. Similarly with the Russians. By declaring their idea, Communism, they oppress others. Whether free America or Communist Russia, both are developing or pushing the self. All our civilization is this pushing out of the self, the expansion and development of the self.

The thought of Hegel, the German philosopher, was recognition of all, acceptance of all; this is all right, that is all right, take this in, take that in. The components of Hegel's dialectic are *thesis, antithesis*, and *synthesis*. Thesis is the fact of the current status quo. The new element opposing the current thesis is the antithesis. Putting together the thesis and the antithesis makes the synthesis. This is the process of life. This is the process of the condition of society. This is the process of progress. Hegel's thought is not denying a thing. Take everything and that develops itself in the process of thesis, antithesis, and synthesis.

Kierkegaard's thought, on the other hand, was selecting one thing and denying all others. That is the basis of his existentialism, taking a certain thing and affirming it and denying others. Hegel and Kierkegaard represent two methods of a way of life. Kierkegaard denied all, but affirmed the existence of God. So, too, with Kant. Immanuel Kant, the foremost philosopher of Germany, denies everything in his "Critique of Pure Reason." However, in his affirmative practical side of it, at the end it was affirmation of God.

Carlyle, the English philosopher, for his significant way of life, said that complete negation is complete affirmation. This seems very close to the way Buddha taught. So, too, Nishida, the outstanding philosopher of Japan, presented the same perspective of understanding: complete negation is complete affirmation.

In Buddhism, especially in the Prajnaparamita sutra, non-ego is taught. Often, the terminology sunyata or void or nothingness or suchness indicates complete negation, nothingness. In the Prajnaparamita sutra, negation is also negated. If there is anything affirmative besides negation, it is not negation. So in the Prajnaparamita sutra, negation is also negated. To me, this negative attitude is very important. In the West, everything is the way of affirmation, while in much of Asian culture, the general way of expression and understanding is through negation. Affirmation limits itself. Only through negation can the comprehensive truth or absolute be expressed.

We are so habituated in the West: we do not want to be negative, we do not want to be passive; we always want to be aggressive, positive, active, and dynamic. In the East, the attitude is more passive, more negative, and more static; but this static quality or negativeness is not relative to positiveness or affirmation. The Buddhist negation is that negation itself is negated.

Kierkegaard and Kant negated everything with the one exception that they affirmed God. Negating all and establishing something, this is not negation in the Buddhist sense. The Buddhist way is that negation is also negated. Nothing is affirmed, but all is negated. That there is no affirmation is the real affirmation. Continuous change is permanence. Samsara is Nirvana; Nirvana is Samsara. The continuous flow of water is the river. That complete negation is complete affirmation is to say continual change is itself permanency.

Shinshu teaches "other-power," denying the self and relying on other-power. This is a very dangerous way of understanding: negating the self and finding the other power. No, it is not two things. There is no other power besides this self. The very negation of the self is the other power.

Most people understand this as negating or denying the self and then finding the other power. Denying the self and depending on the other power, that is dualistic. It is not that kind of negation, but the very negation is affirmation. When self is lost, there is the other power. Without losing self, there is no other power. The losing is the other power. Negation is not compared with or opposed to affirmation. Non-ego or non-self or nothingness is not compared with or opposed to something that is. Higan, the "other" shore, is not over there as compared with here, but Higan is here. When this self is lost, there is the true self. Higan to me is this non-ego self; it is the life of no ego and no selfishness. Higan, of course, is not a geographical place, there, the other shore, nor a conceptual world as compared with this world. This very life, when we transcend the ego self, the transcending itself is non-ego.

We speak of unity, the unity of two things. That is not true unity. For example, it is considered that wife and husband are united into one harmonious life. That is the general Western concept of unity—that wife as an individual and husband as an individual are put together into unity, oneness. But Buddhist oneness is not that kind of oneness. When the husband loses his ego, the husband himself, or when the wife loses her ego, the wife herself, when all is lost, there is oneness. Oneness is not putting together into one. But when everything is lost into nothingness, that is oneness. Not uniting, but *losing*. Complete negation is complete affirmation.

Our tendency is to dichotomize everything, and then try to make unity, harmony between the two. There will be no harmony when you put two things together. Only when you lose yourself do you find yourself. This is the basic understanding of Buddhism: sunyata or nothingness or suchness. "Jiriki wo suteru": throw away all self power. The very act of losing the self power is the other power.

In Buddhist expression, too, there are two ways to look at things. (Of course, we are living in this spatial world; we are living in the world of time, so we have to see things in relation. But relationship is not the true thing.) But, as I was saying, Buddhism has two ways to understand things. One is Hegel's way—accepting everything, all things are all right. This we call "shōju," meaning nothing is thrown away, everything is good, everything is beautiful and valuable, everything has its place, and so we take everything, denounce nothing. This is also called "shōju mon," the gate of "shōju," meaning to take everything in.

The second way that Buddhists have of understanding things is "shaku buku." The gate of "shaku buku" is that of selecting one thing and denying all others. Honen Shonin, the teacher of Shinran, said "Senjaku hongan," meaning accept hongan and cast all other things away. This "senjaku hongan" or choose hongan ("hongan" is often translated as "original vow," which I do not think conveys the true meaning), means to select the true life and deny others. To say this seems dualistic. But selecting the truth alone is in itself denying the false; it is one thing, not two. Selection of the truth *is* denial of the false. Honesty means there is no lie. You do not quit the lie and establish the truth. No, that is not it. It is simultaneous oneness.

That is why one is many and many are one, as is said in Buddhism. I am all and all are I. Such an undivided, non-dualistic, non-ego world is Higan to me. When I examine myself, I see that I am full of ego. All the problems, miseries, unhappiness, uneasiness are ego; it is nothing but ego. If you have any troubles in your life, any worries in your life, it is nothing but your ego. Ego creates problems, miseries, and sufferings. Ego creates attachment and clinging.

At a recent Asoka meeting, one of the members said to me, "You know, Reverend, some time ago you wrote an article on non-attachment in the *Bulletin*. I always carry that article with me, and it has saved me so many times. I have many problems, and when I reflect, I see that they are my attachment to my friends, to money, to certain words my friends say—all the miseries I undergo are my attachment; they are my ignorance. And your article on non-attachment—I don't know how many times it helped me—it's all crushed in the bottom of my purse; still I carry it. I just wanted to let you know how much I appreciate that small article." I do not remember when I wrote that article or even what I said. I had forgotten it all. But at one time I must have felt non-attachment as very helpful to me, so my expression, my experience of that, written on paper, helped some other people. I had no intention of teaching others; I was simply expressing myself. But because our life is one, that helped others. The way I suffer is the same way you suffer and the same way Shakyamuni Buddha suffered; and he solved it, as did Shinran, as did my teacher. They lived life. Their life itself is teaching. Just as when the sun shines, we all get the benefit. The sun is not conscious of giving benefit. It never has realized any altruistic motives, nor thought, "I am shining." It simply shines. Life is like that, too. To me, Ohigan is this non-ego self. The more I find ego in me, the more meaning I find in Higan. It is not non-ego as apart from ego, but in the very fact of realizing my ego, I reach non-ego, the Higan.

So, to me, Higan is very valuable for my own reflections on the teachings. And, this year, Higan means non-ego to me, the life of non-ego. But, of course, Higan, as usually taught, is the six paramitas: sharing, observing the precepts, patience, effort, meditation, and wisdom. These are the six virtues or six perfections. If you take them seriously, each one of them leads into non-ego, selflessness. Selflessness is Higan, the world of Buddha, the world of Nembutsu, the world of oneness—complete negation which is complete affirmation. This is true life, suchness, O-Higan.

THE GREATEST GIFT TO MOTHER

May 13th is Mother's Day. This day is specially set aside to pay tribute to our mothers, though we should not forget them on any day. It is needless to describe the greatness of motherhood and the untold debt of gratitude we owe our mothers. Even when we try to do so, our words seem weak and insufficient though our effort is endless. It is said in the Shinjikan-gyo, one of the Buddhist sutras: "Through the love of kind father and merciful mother, men and women are all peaceful and happy. The love of father is higher than the mountain and mother's love is deeper than the ocean." Then in the Daijukyo (sutra) it is said: "Should there be no Buddha to serve, to serve well your parents is to serve Buddha well."

Indeed, we have to try to realize the vastness of our debt to our parents. Too often we take things for granted. Though we do owe so much to our parents, too often we treat it as a matter of course. More than that we complain, and some people make their parents suffer. Rennyo Shonin once said: "When we become habituated, we do things with our feet, whereas we should do them reverently with our hands. We should be watchful."

We should always do our best for our mothers; but what is "our best"? I believe that our best is to see to it that mother has no cause to worry and that her expectations about us are fulfilled. "We received our bodies from our parents," said Confucius; "to care for the body, and not harm it, is the beginning of filial piety; to become independent and pursue one's life work, and to leave one's name to posterity, is the end of piety."

Whether our mothers are living or dead, to give them no cause for worry is the great thing; however, we let our mothers worry.

Every mother brings up her child with tender care, and with thoughts that the child will be a good boy or girl and become the finest type of man or woman, playing a worthy role in society. Every one of us should remember mother's loving care and hopes, and fulfill her expectations.

Mothers are always thinking of us and worrying about us. The story of Johnny's mother is a true story. It is one of the examples. Mrs. Yamada always stood on the dark, cold porch of her farm house in central California when her son drove away in his vegetable truck. She stood there until the truck's lights disappeared on the distant highway. It was seldom that she went back to bed after Johnny went to market with the produce.

As usual one morning at 3 o'clock, Johnny and his mother ate breakfast together and he drove away in the truck. His mother saw him off from the back porch as usual.

Soon after he left, Johnny discovered that he had forgotten an important paper. He parked his truck and cut across the ranch on foot. As he approached the house he noticed a dark figure in a corner of the porch near a window. He stopped and watched the figure for a few minutes. It did not move. He gathered courage and approached the porch, and said, "Who is there?" There came a reply. "Is that you, Johnny?" As Johnny came to his mother, she took his hand and there was silence. After wiping away her tears, the mother softly said, "Johnny, this is not the first time for me to be standing here. Every morning I stand here long after your truck's lights disappear yonder, hoping that you will be safe and you will not be tempted by gamblers and drinking friends. Of course, I always trust you and have confidence in you, but I worry because there are many temptations and it is easier to go down than up. Johnny, you will never disappoint me?"

The mother was aware that lately Johnny had been drinking and gambling. After this incident, Johnny became a different person and he stayed away from his drinking and gambling companions.

Some of us are fortunate to have our mothers living and some are unfortunate to have lost our mothers. Whether our mothers are living or not, we honor them just the same.

On Mother's Day, those of us whose mothers have passed on recall tender memories of her and try to live the kind of life she taught us; and those of us whose mothers are still with us give dinners or gifts and try our best to make them happy. However, among all gifts, comfort and assurance, and fulfillment of mother's expectations are the greatest gifts we can offer her.

INTROSPECTIONS

On my desk I have a little round stone which I picked up along the creek near the Heart Mountain Relocation Center, Wyoming, where I spent the early years of the recent war. It is a common stone with no value as a jewel; it could be found just anywhere. Yet, to me this common and insignificant stone is a source of great inspiration, a great teacher and a companion as well as a memory of the camp life.

In this round stone, I feel a peaceful, harmonious and perfect character—a character acquired through many years of hardships. As I feel its smoothness and roundness, I know that it was not so in the beginning. It must have had many sharp corners when it was cracked off from the mother stone and began its long journey down the rivers and creeks enduring the heat, the rainstorms and the freezing Wyoming winter. For how long, it is hard to tell, perhaps for thousands of years; and as it was rolled and tossed with the other rocks and stones, it was polished and the sharp corners disappeared. And today as I admire its round and smooth beauty, I know that it took many thousands of years, not just one day, to become round and smooth. Beneath its simple beauty, I perceive a wonderful character.

As I go my way down the creek of life, this stone teaches me patience and endurance. It teaches me to make the best of situations as they come, to accept and ride my waves of karma, for many things that occur are beyond the limit of my power.

In this way, I find peace and contentment from the sufferings of life. As I see many sharp corners and roughness in me, I feel that I am much smaller and inferior to the stone. This little stone on my desk is, indeed, a great teacher to me.

All our sufferings in this world are caused by our ignorance. The very depth of ignorance is not to know oneself. We always feel hindrances and obstructions in our dealing with things and affairs, because we do not know ourselves, and this is the cause for our sufferings and pains. Many people think that the causes of most of our troubles in many cases are in the other people or due to the system of society or to the social environment. But this view considers man as a skeleton, forgetting the spiritual side. Man is not merely existing physically and is not influenced mechanically by other things as physical matters. Our spirit has a power to bring peace and ease upon any circumstance. We can make all existing things, physical and spiritual, to have their worthy places. All persons, things, and circumstances can contribute to beautifying or refining our lives through our introspection and right understanding. We should not live by the irritation or reflex of our peripheral nerves.

If we are clear with ourselves, we will never feel hindrances or sufferings from environmental things and affairs regardless of the condition. Therefore, as the path to alleviate the sufferings of mankind, Buddha tells us the true nature of our character; and to know our character is the highest wisdom. The wisdom to know ourselves is our virtue.

NON-ATTACHMENT

Non-attachment is one of the very important teachings of Buddhism. In fact, the life of Enlightenment is the way of non-attachment. Most of life's troubles are caused by attachment. We get angry, worry, become greedy, complain ignorantly, and have all sorts of complexes. All these causes of unhappiness, tension, stubbornness, and sadness are due to attachment. If you have any trouble or worry, investigate yourself and you will find that the cause is attachment.

There is a famous Zen story of a master and his student. They were on their way to the next village when they came to a swollen stream, where a beautiful young lady stood on the bank trying to get across. The Zen master offered to help her, and lifting her in his arms, carried her to the other shore. They then went their separate ways. The student was greatly puzzled since he had always been taught by the Zen master that a monk should never get near a woman, never touch a woman. The student brooded and brooded about this, and on their return to their temple, he could contain himself no longer and said to the master, "Master, in spite of your daily teachings to the contrary, you held that beautiful young lady at the bank of the stream in your arms today." The master replied, "You fool, I left the girl back there on the shore. Are you still carrying her?"

Non-attachment is not detachment or indifference or escape. We should not become indifferent to life's problems. Life should not be escaped; it cannot be escaped if one is sincere. Life and its problems must be squarely faced and dealt with, but they are not things to become attached to. It is true that money has its importance, but one who becomes attached to it becomes a miser and a slave to money. It is so easy to become attached to our own beauty, ability, or possessions so that we come to feel superior. It is equally easy to become attached to our own homeliness, inability, or poverty so that we come to feel inferior. Attachment to favorable conditions leads to greed and false optimism while attachment to adverse conditions leads to resentment and pessimism. Certainly, our attachment to things, conditions, feelings, and ideas is much more troublesome than we realize.

We even become attached to our sickness when we fall ill. It is better not to do so. All sickness will be cured, except one which is death. When sick, be sick, and do your best for recovery. Accept and transcend, or, better, accept-transcend. Life is changing; all things are changing; all conditions are changing. So let things go. All abuse, anger, criticism—let them come and let them go. Whatever we do, we should do sincerely, honestly, and with full strength; and when it is done, it is done. Do not become attached to it. Many people become attached to the past or to the future, and neglect the important present. We must live the best "now," with full responsibility.

When the sun shines, enjoy it; when it rains, enjoy it. All things in life, let them come and let them go. This is a secret of life that keeps one from getting upset or being neurotic. The Buddha says that all things in life and in the world are in constant change, so do not become attached to them.

THE LIFE OF BECOMING

The word "becoming" is the participle of "become," grammatically speaking, and commonly has the meaning of "to change into" or "to come to be," as a caterpillar becomes a butterfly or an acorn becomes an oak tree. As an adjective it means appropriate, suitable or proper. This is all in the material world. The life of becoming is a becoming in the spiritual world. It is the continual revealing of truth in our lives and in all things. Truth is forever revealing itself in all forms and in all phases of life—this is the spiritual becoming; it is the continual truth and becoming truth within truth in our spiritual world. This is not in the past or future; it is life here and now in this present world, fulfilling its purpose, realizing its value and revealing its beauty. Real happiness is always in the state of becoming because truth is always in the becoming. And in this becoming there is freedom and naturalness; no artificiality. Also, there is creativeness, for as we live in the truth we are creating new life within us. And there is permanency because eternal becoming is eternity and it is the breath of life. This is the Dharma itself, the Buddha's life. It is the true

Buddhist life where beauty, truth and happiness are revealed and enjoyed.

This life of becoming, the living in the continual truth, is in the present. Happiness is in the present, and only by living in the present is real happiness achieved. Actually in the world of truth there is only the present, but people tend to live in three worlds, past, present, and future. In spite of living in the present, some people live more in the past and others more in the future. Older people, generally speaking, tend to live more in the past. "Ah, the good old days" or "When I was young" are familiar phrases heard. On the other hand, young people tend to live more in future hopes. Recalling happy memories and planning for the future are part of life, but becoming attached to the past or future and forgetting to live in the present brings unhappiness and disharmony. Living in the present is most important. This immediate present is what we must be most concerned with. Are we happy? Are we free, now, from idle complaints, greediness, frustrations, and hatred? Attachment to the past makes a person stubborn, and attachment to the future may cause idealist illusions and disappointments.

It is the Buddha's teaching that all things are in constant change. The truth of life is becoming; in fact, everything is becoming. The truth and beauty of nature are in this change. Trees and flowers are beautiful because they change. Suppose a tree stopped growing. It would mean its death.

Growth is change; it is life itself. It is the unfolding of internal life. The budding and growing of new leaves, blooming of flowers, spreading of summer leaves, and falling of leaves in autumn are all beautiful. The entire life of a tree is the life of becoming. There is growth and life.

Human life is no exception in the world of nature. We must constantly grow, individually and collectively. Why is it that the wonderful Greek culture came to its end and the great Roman civilization fell in ruin? It was stagnation. Why does love so often end in failure? Why are so many homes destroyed? Because couples forget to cultivate love. After a few years of marriage, they forget how to love. Divorces occur mostly in this so-called period of fatigue in married life. It is all because love is left to become stagnant.

Now, let us take the example of time. Time is a continuous flow. It never stops. In this continuous flow there is eternity. Buddha said, "In this very transiency, immortality is hidden." A river is another example. It is nothing but a continuous flow of water. Without this flow there is no river. Flowers are beautiful because they bloom to their fullness and fall when they should, without clinging to the tree; children are lovely because they grow.

In this changing world or world of becoming, if we refuse to change, there comes struggle, suffering, war. To be born is certainly becoming, but death also is becoming. There is a wonderful philosophy in this life of becoming. We have to accept all changes that come and be ever born anew. A child has its cuteness, youth its vigor, and old age its place of respect. Each has his own beauty and each beauty has its place.

In each time, in each place, in each life, there is the absolute value and beauty. Every moment is living and it is a natural life. Living in the truth is the Buddha's world and in this Buddha's world there is naturalness. Shinran Shonin said "Jinen Hōni," which means to be natural according to the Dharma, the law.

When we observe the world of nature, we see beauty blooming forth in its fullness, freely and naturally without any attachment whatsoever. Change is accepted, and by accepting is the truth and beauty revealed. In the truth of life, everything is becoming. So it is in our life, if we remain free from selfish ego attachments and live the life of naturalness, we live in the true sense of living.

In true living there is creativeness which makes life meaningful and gives it its value. As we live we must constantly create, constantly grow spiritually, or we will be merely existing. When we live in the life of truth or in Buddha's world or in the life of becoming, we are living a creative life.

And in this creative life there is no artificiality and no mere change. Artificial or pretended friendship or love in any human relationship cannot bring happiness, only suffering and misery and a constrained and uncomfortable life. No matter how beautiful and excellent the imitation may be, there is no truth in it. Like the artificial flower, it is beautiful, but we tire of it soon. A clock ticks the time, but it is not the life of becoming or creating.

In our life we can be moving, yet not creating. It all depends upon the thoughts and purpose behind the motion. Walking the sidewalk without a purpose has no meaning; however, walking on it to go to school or to see one's sweetheart is quite meaningful and there is joy and purpose.

So with our life, we must pause to analyze whether we are merely moving about each day or are living a creative life. If we can not find beauty, joy, happiness and value in our life, then we are not living the life of becoming. It is existing and not actually living.

To live is a dynamic force; this means to be one with the Universal Law, to express the Buddha-nature within, to reveal truth through our personalities. A religious life, living in oneness with Buddha's teachings, is a creative life in which everything becomes meaningful. Each man, each thing, good or bad has meaning and, all will be a source of guidance to us to a thankful and a creative life.

As we live in this great life of becoming, we live in the life of Nembutsu, the religious life wherein Buddha and we are one. In the Nembutsu we see and feel Buddha everywhere and in everything. Life itself becomes the unfolding of Buddha. The life of naturalness and the life of creativeness are summarized in this life of Nembutsu, which is the life of respect and humbleness through which the whole world and life become the Buddha's world. It is a marvelous world of adoration and it is ever creating and becoming.

FREEDOM

All men seek happiness, peace and freedom. Where freedom is, there is happiness and peace; therefore, freedom is the basic desire of man. Freedom is the opposite of control, limitation, bondage, and ignorance.

Buddhism teaches the way of freedom, which is Enlightenment or Nirvana. The purpose of Buddhism is the attainment of Nirvana, which is a life of freedom. Man is not free as long as he is bound by time and space.

Everyone fears death and does not want to die. Yet, we all die without exception. Why do we fear death? Death is a natural thing. It is a process of life just as much as birth is. We need not fear death. When flowers are past their bloom, it is only natural for them to scatter. When leaves are matured in their growth, they turn color and fall. If you transcend death, then you are free from birth and death. In the life of truth we do not die. Death does not hinder our true life. There is no fear of death in the true man. Man is free from birth and death when he attains Nirvana. Nirvana is the world of freedom.

Man fears punishment or consequences. Punishment or consequence is the law of karma. No one can escape from karma. It is a natural consequence. If you are born, you will die. Birth includes death. All that is made is subject to decay. Man tries to avoid or escape from inevitable things. This is evidence of ignorance. Accept the inevitable things, not unwillingly, but willingly and naturally. When you accept willingly, when it is not forced upon you, you are free. Acceptance is your freedom. Acceptance is transcendence. Transcendence means acceptance. Transcendence and acceptance are not two things but one and the same. Here exists freedom. If you are short, accept the shortness and do not let anything hinder you. You can excel in many things. If one is born as Japanese, be a good Japanese. Roses are red, the sky is blue, snow is white, sugar is sweet, and pepper is hot. That is the way it should be. All things are good and all are free as they are. You need not compare. Everyone has his place in the world. So be it. Flowers are red and leaves are green. This is the world of suchness—the free and natural world.

Buddhism teaches Enlightenment, which is the opposite of ignorance. Enlightenment is freedom, and ignorance is bondage. Enlightenment is to see things as they are. Upon seeing a rope on the road in the evening, and thinking that it is a snake, you become scared; but if you are able to see the rope as a rope under better light, there is no fear. If one is able to see things as they are, he is free. Ignorance is the cause of all troubles. We do many stupid things because of our ignorance. To be greedy, to get angry, to have idle complaints—all these causes of suffering are the results of ignorance. To be free or to attain freedom is to overcome ignorance, and that is enlightenment.

We often think that others hinder our own freedom. The wife blames her husband and the husband blames his wife. Often we blame society and condemn the "system." But it is not the environment that makes you miserable or deprives you of your freedom. No matter how good the environment is, unless your mind is free, you can not be a free person. One person said that he wanted to be free; however, when a red light signal at a crossing stopped him, he felt that he was not free. To me, the red light is not a hindrance. I do not want to go against the light because it is dangerous. I work because I want to work, not because I have to work. I help people because I want to help, not because I have to help.

This world is free. Our life is free. This world is the world of Nirvana. Nirvana is not something we attain or grasp. Rather, we discover ourselves in the world of Nirvana, the true free world in which we are living. Nirvana is right here, now. Heaven and hell are not places we go after we die. They are here now. They are the contents of our own life. We create a heaven-like or hell-like place. We are responsible. It is our ignorance that makes our whole world dark. When we are enlightened, the whole world becomes bright.

It is not the devil that brings darkness and misery, nor gods that bring happiness or brightness. It is up to us to make our life bright or dark, to be free or to be in bondage. Freedom exists in us. Freedom does not exist in the relative and comparative world but only in the world of oneness, the absolute. Only when subject and object become one, is there freedom.

LIVING LIFE

Living life is everyone's concern and is the most important concern. I wonder how many people are really living life. Are you living or merely existing? The real joy and peace of life are based on living life. As we welcome a new year, I would like to look into this important matter of life.

As I see it, many people who are impatient, nervous, always complaining, tired, bored, and indifferent are not living life. On the contrary, one who is living life is bright, vibrant, creative and unfolding from within, and he feels the meaning of life and enjoys his work.

One day Buddha came to a certain village where he saw three bricklayers working. He asked one, "What are you doing?" The answer was, "I am laying bricks." Buddha then asked the second man what he was doing. He answered, "I am making money." When Buddha went to the third man and asked him what he was doing, the third man looked at the Buddha and said, "I am building a temple." His face was bright and full of hope. He was living.

Rev. Saito translated Kenji Miyazawa's "The Elements of an Outline for the Farmer's Art" with Joan Sweany, and it is printed in this month's *Suchness*. Kenji Miyazawa really lived life. He lived in the northern part of Japan where life was hard and poor; famine continued, and the young farmers left one by one. Miyazawa stood amidst the farmers as a farmer and proposed with his life that the only way to save the farmers (and, in turn, save oneself and mankind) is to find "The Farmer's Art," as the true meaning of life for them. Unless farmers realize the true meaning of life as farmers, they cannot live on their farms. The true life is an art. Everyone, whether farmer, factory worker, teacher, or doctor, must become an artist of life. Kenji Miyazawa lived the farmer's art, and he was an artist of life as a farmer.

Only when one lives his life does he know its meaning, and compensation for his work is not necessary because work itself is the compensation. The work is fulfillment of life itself; therefore, there is meaning and joy of life regardless of the condition, time, and place.

All must live life—his own life. But this very personal life is not just isolated and independent. The true life is always one with the universal life, yet is uniquely independent at the same time. The true life is never sacrificing nor being sacrificed. The true life is always creative and unfolds from within. Therefore, it is an art of life. One is an artist of life whatever one's occupation is.

In a garden there are roses, gladioli, marigolds, lilies, and cosmos. They are all independently beautiful; yet together, in harmony, they also make the whole garden beautiful and in each separate season. Some grow tall, some climb and others creep; all have their places and each is beautiful in its place. There is no superiority complex nor inferiority complex. There is no envy or jealousy. Life just fulfills itself. Life is sometimes tough and sometimes soft. Life just is. Be it.

Red flowers have red light yellow flowers have yellow light, green flowers have green light, and white flowers have white light. When life is put on canvas, it becomes beautiful art; when it is manifested in rhythm, it becomes inspiring music; when put into words, it is a beautiful poem. Capital and labor are both important in industry. One cannot say which is more important. Both are equally important. Piano and wastebasket, parlor and bathroom, all are equally important. Garbage collector, street repairman, doctor, and merchant—all are important. All must respect each other. Each one must shine where he is and as he is. Each one must be the best without any comparison. Each one must live his life. Do not be impatient; forget self-pity. Live life. Be the artist of your own life. When we live life, there is no argument, no discussion. There is only life—living and shining.

NATURALNESS

What can we learn from the life of Shinran? He was a great religious teacher and we can learn many things from his life. One of his teachings is the life of naturalness.

Shinran used the word "jinen hōni" to express naturalness. "Jinen" means nature and "hōni" means according to the law of life. It is the understanding of things and the naturalness of life. By the life of "jinen hōni" one ceases to worry needlessly and lives naturally. My friend Rev. Kenryo Kanamatsu wrote a book, *Naturalness*. It is a wonderful book. I wish everyone would read it. Our life has become very artificial and superficial; we must come down to earth and be natural. All the poems of Japan and China express the reality or impressions of human life and they always end in unity with nature.

Only when we become one with nature will we be able to solve our problems. When one attains perfect harmony with nature, he becomes one with it. It is to live like the blooming of the flowers, the shining of the sun. It is to be truly oneself. This is naturalness. Children are cute because they are natural; they do not pretend or show artificiality.

To be one with nature is not to worry needlessly and wish things were different from what they are. It is to face reality and live life truthfully. Of course, we have many worries and we have to make plans, but there is just so much a man can do. In the end, things must harmonize with nature. It is a great mistake to say "Conquer it," for we can never conquer nature; we can only harmonize with it. Shinran called this "jinen hōni," to follow the law of the Dharma, the teachings, to live with the Dharma itself, the source of inner peace.

The life of naturalness goes beyond petty human worries and doubts. Nature takes care of itself. In the medical world we have made great advances, but there is a limit to what doctors and medicine can do. We can only harmonize with nature, for nature itself must cure. All our efforts are a supplement to nature and its workings.

Shinran did not worry needlessly about life. He lived in the flow of life, the flow of nature which he called "tariki," the other power, or "hongan," the essence of life. Life has its own principle of operation, and there is really just so much we can do within our power. Japanese people say "makasu," which means to let the principle work itself.

Rev. Kiyozawa said, "Who am I? I am nothing but this moment in the flow of life. This flow of life is not within my control; it is the life of the universe itself. The life of the universe flows in me and I just flow with this life and that is myself." Indeed, we have to make plans, we have to make an effort, we have to do numerous things according to the way we live; but, in the last analysis, it is not our own doing but Life's doing. I think modern people have too many worries about things. Many people are overly concerned about the number of calories they consume at every meal. If people think more about their blessings than about their calories, life will be much happier and more peaceful. We worry too much about the petty things of life. We should do whatever must be done and be one with it and not worry about it. Let life take care of itself; let the true life flow out from within and be free. To Shinran, every day was the best life, for at every moment life flowed from within. No pretense, no false front was necessary. He was sincere and earnest in living himself as he was. Many of us, do we not worry because we are hiding something? We live a double life and thus there is worry. If we are as we are, we live as we are without pretending, without superficiality. No false front, and life will be at ease.

The life of naturalness is a life of freedom, a life where there is no need of useless worry, a life where there is complete oneness with the law of nature—not conquering but harmonizing. It is a life of no artificiality or superficiality. Modern man has too many masks to wear. We must unmask and be ourselves, sincerely, earnestly, and live truly as we are. I think this teaching is Shinran's great contribution to us all.

SERENITY

Snow scene on a quiet morning, a calm lake, a walk in autumn woods, smoke from a single incense stick at morning meditation, listening to the simmering sound of the kettle in a tea room—serenity from these scenes or moments is something beyond words.

Serenity is the home of our spiritual life. From this tranquil mind many deep thoughts and dynamic actions will arise. Indeed, serenity is the home of creativity and the source of real peace and happiness of life.

Therefore, to create serenity in life is very important, particularly for city dwellers like ourselves. Modern urbanization, external expansion, increasing mechanization increase the complexity and diminish the serenity of our lives.

Some people just cannot be quiet, cannot sit still. Some people leave the radio or television on all day long though they are not really listening; it is a matter of habit, and they cannot stand quietness. These people are nervous and are irritated by trivial things and upset so easily. They cannot see life as it is or things as they are.

To be calm or serene means uneasiness and boredom to many people. The great consumption of sleeping tablets and tranquilizers is a symptom of the lack of inner serenity. These external, objective applications and attitudes supersede the internal aspects of life. Whether good or bad, we look for outside things and neglect to see them within us.

To quiet down our irritation and nervousness, many of us chew gum or smoke cigarettes, but this is more or less a temporary method. We need something more fundamental. Perhaps that is the reason why meditation is taught and emphasized in Buddhism.

Meditation is the foundation of Buddhist life. Though all Buddhists, regardless of sects and schools, are taught meditation, Zen particularly emphasizes meditation, while Shin teaches recitation of Nembutsu. I believe all religions teach the meditative way of life because calmness and serenity are essential to a good life. All prayers have this efficacy. Ralph Waldo Emerson said that everyone should have 10 or 15 minutes to himself, alone, each day. If all Americans meditated 10 minutes each day, America would be changed.

Only when we are calm, are we able to see things as they really are. Only when our minds are tranquil, are we able to reflect the truth—just as the calm surface of water reflects the beautiful moon. A disturbed or unsettled mind cannot see the truth of things, just as wavy, disturbed water cannot reflect the moon. All creative things—poetry, art, philosophy—are the products of serene and composed minds, because all require a keen awareness of life, and this awareness is only possible when our life is serene.

Basho, the famous Japanese haiku poet, showed his keen awareness when he wrote:

> *Yoku mireba*   *When I look carefully,*
> *Nazuna hanasaku*   *Nazunas are blooming*
> *Kakine kana.*   *Along the hedge!*

The nazuna is a very common, insignificant little wildflower. "Yoku mireba," when I look carefully, is very important. Unless one is calm and aware, he cannot see carefully or closely. The small wildflower will be overlooked. But, though no one else pays any attention, Basho looks closely and sees the nazunas blooming in their best to the sun! How exquisite they are. How fortunate he feels. The mystery and wonder of life are all there. Basho could not help speaking to them. How wonderful and honorable they are, so humble, yet with their own glory and pride. "Kakine kana," along a hedge. The nazunas were blooming along a common, old hedge, with no one paying any attention. "Kana" has no particular meaning in itself but it is a very important poetical expression. It is spoken exclamation mark and gives an emphasis of poetic feeling.

It is the calm and composed mind that is able to make such keen observations, finding life in anyplace, and tasting the oneness of life in nature. That is the essence of poetry.

Tea ceremony is another good example of learning serenity.

In tea ceremony, we first learn how to walk. We must walk quietly—quietly, but not tip-toe walking. One must walk quietly but firmly. One comes into the tea room very quietly and humbly, bowing through the small entrance. One very attentively observes the scroll painting, the flower arrangement, and every utensil. Serenity and tranquility pervade the entire tea ceremony. The discipline of the tea ceremony teaches the art of serenity, awareness, and grace, which then become part of one's whole life.

While serenity is a part of our life, it must be cultivated. It is just like life—essentially good, but if it is neglected and left alone, it becomes wild. Discipline and cultivation are necessary in life. Serenity must be learned. Meditation, tea ceremony, writing haiku, and Japanese calligraphy are ways to cultivate serenity in life.

NIRVANA

I am often asked about Nirvana. But Nirvana cannot be explained because it is reality and, if I explain it, it will be conceptual and not Nirvana. I can only point to it.

The word—*Nirvana* in Sanskrit, and *Nehan* in Japanese—literally means "extinguished" or "blotted out"; that is to say, the ego is extinguished, the self (our mistaken idea of self) is wiped out. But it is probably better to say that the ego is transcended. Nirvana is the state of realization that this is a selfless and egoless world. The egoless and selfless world is a serene and pure world.

If Nirvana is said to be an egoless, selfless and pure world, then one might think of it as a motionless, dead world apart from what we consider our reality of life. But Nirvana is not separate from the reality of our life and world. Nirvana is both dynamic and static. This may sound contradictory, but Nirvana is the world where contradiction is not contradictory. Real life is static and, at the same time, dynamic.

A candle flame is very static when there is no wind to affect it; but, within that very quiet-looking flame, the crashing events of combustion are taking place. A runner at the starting line of a track meet, just when the starter says, "On your mark; get set..." is at that moment quiet, motionless, but he is ready to take off on the hundred-yard dash. The whole dash is in him; he is alert, and dynamic, though this dynamism appears in static form. The faster a top spins, the more static it looks. As it spins more slowly, it becomes more active; that is, it wobbles tipsily, until it finally comes to a dead stop. Sometimes we see children playing so quietly, not disturbing others; it is because they are so deeply busy, absorbed in their play. These examples should illustrate that the serene quietness of Nirvana is not dead quietness, but very much alive—static and dynamic simultaneously.

Nirvana is explained very negatively by Western scholars or non-Buddhists, because they do not understand Nirvana in its totality. They only see the static or negative side of it. Modern people want to see the dynamic side of life. They think that dynamic, active, progressive, and positive things have modernity. But life has the other side or aspect also. What is life if it does not include death? Life is both life and death. Destruction makes progress possible. There. is activity only because there is passivity. These are relative and complement things. But our dualistic minds always form concepts that attempt to dichotomize things which are not separate from one another in reality. Concepts are not real things; a conceptualized world is a dead world. Living actualities lose their life when put into concepts. Nirvana, the world of true reality, is a living world and it transcends the relative worlds of static or dynamic, good or bad, and life or death.

We modern people become victims of many concepts. We try to understand things conceptually. If a person tries to understand life or love conceptually, he will never understand life or love. Similarly, if one forms concepts of heaven and hell, good and evil, or God and Devil, these become dead, stereotyped things and lose their true meaning. Nirvana is not a concept; it is reality. It is life itself.

Sometimes people speak of "attaining Nirvana." But Nirvana is not something to be attained. The whole world is Nirvana, or is in Nirvana. It is more correct to say that we find ourselves in Nirvana, rather than that we attain Nirvana. Shinran says in his *Jōdo Wasan*, "Tathagata is Nirvana; Nirvana is Buddhahood," "The great true mind is Buddhahood; Buddhahood is Tathagata," and in his *Shōshinge*, he says, "Samsara is Nirvana."

Tathagata means "suchness," the world of suchness, of things as they are. *Samsara* means "everyday life." The whole world is Nirvana, and Nirvana is suchness. Nirvana is everyday life. The world, the everyday world, appears chaotic or peaceful, ugly or beautiful, depending on our own minds. We make the world the way we want to in our minds. An ugly and nervous mind cannot see beauty and peace in the world. Our own world is the reflection of our own minds. It is like seeing the world with colored glasses. If we take off the colored glasses, we will see the world and things as they are. To see things as they are and to understand things as they are is the key to Nirvana. Nirvana is the content of enlightenment. When one becomes enlightened, the world of Nirvana opens.

LIFE WITHOUT REGRET

Regrets are often felt from one's own doings because of the lack of seriousness on one's part. Many things confront us in life and unless correct decisions are made with thorough thinking, regrets are sure to follow.

Especially such things as choosing a life companion, or a career. These problems must be dealt with serious thought and an absolute choice must be made to avoid regrets in later life. Happiness, we must remember, can never be attained if one lives a life full of regrets.

Then how can a life without regrets be attained? It can be done by listening to the inner heart. Whatever the true inner heart says is the right way. Listen to its voice. If you know definitely and clearly what you wish, then it is not difficult to make a decision. And, if you make up your mind, act accordingly with all your might. Place your whole effort, your very life into it, and work for it at the risk of your own life. Then, there cannot be any regrets. Any form of work, if one pays his life's price for it, will be honorable, and no great work can be truly accomplished otherwise.

If one imitates others in settling one's problems, it is likely to bring regrets later. Advices must be considered although they must be only references. You, as an individual, must make the final decision. If you decide upon things according to public opinion, money, external looks or obligations, it will lead you toward regrets.

You must stand upon your own feet and decide for yourself. Where work is concerned, do it whole-heartedly, and even if you die doing it, you know you will have no regrets.

THE CENTER OF LIFE

"I know that we should be thankful to our mothers but I cannot be thankful to my mother, because she did not do much for me. My parents were divorced and I did everything by myself. In fact, my mother gave me more hardships and sufferings than good. What have I to thank her for? How could I?" This statement was made by a very intelligent young man. I asked him whether he is happy as he is now; and further I asked him whether he feels a real joy or gladness in life and is able to say, "I am grateful to be alive." His answer was, "No."

Unless we are thankful to ourselves now, we cannot be thankful to anyone. Even if this young man's mother had done much for him, I do not think that he could really be thankful to her, for he cannot be thankful to himself as he is now. On the other hand, if he found himself, and lived a meaningful and grateful life, he could not help feeling thankful to his mother, who gave him life, regardless of what she has or has not done for him.

In ordinary moral life and modern utilitarian point of view, if someone was kind to us then we express our thankfulness.

This is to say, if we receive some benefit, then we express thanks and appreciation. This kind of human relation is nothing but business-like "give and take."

In the world of truth, religion, and love, it is altogether different. In fact, it is the opposite. The starting point is not mother or any external things but ourselves. If we are saved now, our whole past will be saved. Our "salvation" goes backward into the past. If we find meaning in our lives now, then the whole world becomes meaningful just as when we are cheerful, the whole world is cheerful. The real meaning of "I pledge myself to strive for the Enlightenment of all beings" is the attainment of our own enlightenment. Shinran Shonin said that he did not recite the Nembutsu for his parents, but when he is able to recite the true Nembutsu, he is a worthy son of his parents.

Buddha's world is the world where we transcend the world of duality and become one. To the above-mentioned young man, the problem is not what his mother did but that she is the one who gave him life. His mother and he are not separate in the world of truth; they are one. The world and we are not two but one. The world is you and you are the world. As long as we think dualistically, we will have problems.

ETERNAL PRESENT

Time is a continuation of the present. Today exists only today and it cannot be in the past or in the future. In other words, this "today" does not come again in the eternal future. Today is the most unique, noble and the only "today" in the eternal past and eternal future. It cannot be repeated. Your present life is the only life and your life today cannot be lived again. This very present is not merely present but it is the eternal present.

"Today" is the most important, unique and absolute existence. We live only today because yesterday is already past and tomorrow is yet to come. We want to make this given and important "today" a beautiful, noble, and meaningful "today."

When your present is meaningful, then your past and future become meaningful. To one who is despondent now, his future is also despondent; to one who is grateful now, his past is also grateful. Only when one discovers himself—what he is and what he really wishes to live for—does he find life very significant and appreciate it. Then his entire past becomes significant and grateful and his entire future becomes important, bright, and meaningful.

Thus, without the present, there is no past and there is no future. The present is not merely the continuation of the past nor is the future the continuation of the present. The enlightenment or the salvation of the present is the enlightenment of the past and the future.

Buddha did not speculate into the unknown past as to when, how and who created what. He always lived in the actual present. Neither did he speculate into the unknowable future as to heaven or hell after death. He realized heaven and hell within himself rather than outside of himself. He always lived in the perfection, the enlightenment of the present.

The realization of the eternal present is very important. No matter how much we say of the past or look to the promises of the future, unless we are saved today or have the enlightenment of the present, there is no complete peace and freedom.

ONENESS

Toward the end of this essay, Rev. Kubose uses the term "complexes." His meaning isn't completely clear, but given the time this was written and the context, he seems to be using the term in the Freudian sense. In Freudian psychology, a complex is a cluster of unconscious beliefs, ideas and attitudes that influence someone's emotions and behaviors. It's not unlike the Buddhist concept of Sankharas, except that these are specifically based on ignorance and misunderstanding. --ED

Oneness does not mean that all become one and the same. The recognition of difference is oneness. One is many and many is one. Equality means difference and difference is equality. Everyone is unique in himself, and this uniqueness makes the world interesting. In being unique, there is untold respect for others' uniqueness. Only when one really respects and honors himself, can he respect others. Each one should be as perfect as he himself can be. Each person should be the finest that he himself is—without comparison with others.

A beautiful symphony is possible because of the different

instruments. A garden is beautiful because of the different flowers, shrubs, trees, and rocks. Man and woman harmonize because they are different. Assimilation is not forgetting or losing the uniqueness of individuals, but it is recognition and understanding of others, harmonizing with them. Democracy is lived well when each person understands and recognizes the rights of others and respect others.

No one needs to try to be "just like" anyone else. Whether Japanese, Irish, or from any other culture, we should be the most dignified and honorable and the best that we are. In a Buddhist sutra, it is written that willows are green and flowers are red. Willows are beautiful in their greenness and red flowers are beautiful as red flowers. Another sutra says that red color has red light, white color has white light, yellow color has yellow light. These words express the same thought.

Each day is an absolute day and cannot be substituted for another day; each place is unique and absolute in its place; each person is also unique and absolute. The heaven is above and earth is below; this makes unity, and it is not a question of which is better. Father and mother, husband and wife, man and wife, man and woman—the worthiness of each cannot be judged by comparison. Judging oneself and others by comparison creates complexes.

Complexes are the disease of the modern world. In order to attain peace, harmony and joy, we have to get rid of these complexes. That is to say, we have to see and understand things as they are. Each and all are unique and independent and, at the same time, all are interrelated and interdependent. We are all one.

BEAUTIFY THE MIND

There is an outside and inside to all material things. Some are beautiful only on the outside, while in others the beauty is hidden within. And, of course, there are things that are all beautiful or all ugly. There is an outside and inside in our daily living, too. We like to be praised; therefore, in order to achieve this, we often put up a false front. We do things with selfish motives.

False front is pretended living where, for instance, we do not find true kindness but kindness expecting rewards, clothes being worn in competition or envy, and where people are nice only because they want to be considered nice and not because they cannot help being nice. In such a pretended life, happiness cannot last; there will be complaints and regrets. It seems that people devote so much of their time in beautifying their physical appearances or in achieving praises for their deeds that they forget or ignore beautifying their minds. Always the real self must shine forth in whatever we do. In our work we must put in our utmost and right effort, then no matter what criticisms we hear we know that we have done our best. And, also, if disappointments follow, we receive them and not blame anyone.

How easily we strive only for material happiness and forget that we live through our minds; what we are is the expression of our minds. Let us beautify our minds to enjoy true happiness. Our minds must be beautiful to live in a beautiful world. What we are, the world is. Let us not seek beauty objectively for beauty is within our own minds.

> *"When you reach the heart of life*
> *you shall find beauty in all things, even in the*
> *eyes that are blind to beauty."*
>
> *Kahlil Gibran*

IS LIFE FUN?

At the meeting of Koso Kai, the monthly meeting held on the 27th, the memorial day of my teacher, someone said that life is fun. But life for most people is not fun; it is full of struggles and sufferings. Therefore, much discussion followed.

Perhaps the word "fun" was misleading; if the word "thankful" were used it might not have created such a disagreement. However, no matter what word is substituted, the truth of the statement could not be fully understood unless life's criterion of value changes one hundred eighty degrees through religious awakening.

If we have religious awakening, life can be and will be thankful in spite of all adversities, and all adversities are good and natural. In this way we will transcend our troubles instead of trying to escape from them. More than transcending them, our very troubles, sufferings and adversities will become the causes for our thankfulness. If we have religious awakening, life is viewed objectively and we can say that life is "fun." Even death can be faced calmly without fear. When life is viewed philosophically and religiously, there are no regrets, no worries and no fears. In our religious awakening, we see through the eye of wisdom and all is justified and everything is all right. We realize that our sufferings are caused by our ignorance.

Let me tell you a true story. There was a mother who suffered terribly, because she had an abnormal child. Although she was well-educated and a very intelligent woman, she was deeply disturbed to have such a child. Her life was full of complaints and hatred toward herself and also toward her family. At times her hatred made her want to kill the child.

One day a Zen priest who had frequently visited the family called on the mother. That day she complained more than usually to the priest. She said boldly that if only the child did not exist, she could be happy. The priest looked at her and said sternly, "What kind of a devil are you? You are killing your child and hurting yourself and everybody in the family. Don't you know that this boy is a Buddha and you are the mother who gave birth to this Buddha? Your child came to you to teach you a religious life, the way of the Buddha. Instead of complaining you should be thankful to this child and respect him." The mother was startled and dumbfounded by the stern admonition of the priest. She listened in silence as the priest continued, "A person like you who possesses such selfish and arrogant pride will never become religious or understand the life of humbleness, patience, and gratitude. Your child is teaching us a life of appreciation and gratitude. Everytime you place your child in front of your store in his buggy, people who pass by see the child and they are taught or reminded to be grateful that they are normal."

From that day on the mother began to think on the spiritual side of life and found a deeper meaning in life and things. For the first time she realized that she has been living by the mere external appearance of things and began to live a thankful and blessful life. Life is indeed full of sufferings and full of complaints until we begin to see the truth about life with our spiritual eye. If we have a philosophic view and religious awakening, we are able to transcend petty things and find that life is "fun." In viewing our life objectively, we are able to rise above our mistakes and smallness of ourselves, and thus be able to laugh at our own anger, greediness, and idle complaints. In our religious awakening, we should be big enough to accept all troubles with courage and a smile.

WATER

In the sūtras we find that the Buddha often uses the example of water. Water changes its form according to the shape of the receptacle in which it is put, but it never changes its essence or nature.

When water is put into a round bowl, it becomes round. Water is not stubborn, as some men are; it adapts itself according to the situation. Yet, at the same time it remains water and never changes its own essence.

Water is very humble. It always seeks the lowest level. It never tries to be on top or show off but goes to the bottom. The lowest level is the most safe, natural and peaceful place. Water is soft and meek, yet it has a very dynamic power that can turn great dynamos and can break great concrete walls and dikes. Water devastates a village as flood; it chews up the granite by the seaside; dropping from an eave, it can drill a hole in stone. Yet, it is a most soft and faithful thing.

It is the calmest and most peaceful thing on a calm morning on the bay. I always admire Lake Michigan as I drive along Lake Shore Drive. Some mornings the lake is quite calm and restful and beautiful. But the same lake shows a most fearful rage, dashing against the rocks of the shore. Yet, there is no intention nor any artificiality in water.

Water does not pretend. When it gets hot enough, it becomes steam, and when it gets cold enough, it freezes. When it becomes ice or steam, it is not water any more, and it does not function as water. But it tends to return to its original form as water. Water is so versatile, according to its nature.

Water is the source of all life. Without it, there is no life. When things are wet, we say "It is wet and messy" and we dislike it, but the very wetness is the important thing in life. So, in our life, many troubles and hardships are disliked things, but the very troubles are life itself. If there is no trouble, there is no life.

The mind of Buddha is often said to be a great ocean-mind. Buddha's mind is large enough to receive and accept all things and everything and purify them all, just as the ocean receives all the dirty waters of rivers and purifies them all. If we have a great ocean mind, we will take in all things and will not be upset by them. There is no tension and no complex of any kind in the great-ocean-mind. We can meditate much on water, and, indeed, we can learn many things from it.

A STONE

A man stumbled over a stone which upset him greatly. The cause of his stumbling was the stone. Therefore, the cause of anger and misery which was produced by his stumbling was completely outside of him. If there were no stone in his path, he might not have stumbled; hence, no anger or misery would have resulted.

This logic seems quite correct. However, many people pass the same path. Some of them stumble over the stone and others do not. Those who do see the obstruction are able to avoid the trouble.

Thus, the cause of anger and misery really lies in this man who did not see the stone. He himself is the cause of trouble because he did not or was unable to see the stone. A man who observes and is careful is free from stumbling. Therefore, the cause of trouble is carelessness, blindness and ignorance.

This analysis shows the difference between a religious and non-religious person. A religious person from Buddhist point of view always sees the cause of misery or happiness just as a scientist looks into the cause of things. Religion begins from introspection. Without self-introspection there is no religion. Buddhism teaches the truth about life and world and the causes of miseries and troubles of life. It teaches how to understand and to face and transcend human miseries and troubles.

In our life there are many troubles which we stumble over. A man stumbles over a stone and scorns to find a stone in the middle of the road and he blames someone for leaving it there. A man says that he is deceived and blames the deceiver, but some are not deceived no matter how much others try to deceive them. A wise and alert person is not deceived. Those who are gullible or greedy are easily deceived. Here again, we see the cause of deception is in the one who is deceived rather than the one who tries to deceive. A husband thinks that his wife is the cause of his unhappiness and, contrarily, the wife thinks that the husband is the cause of her troubles. This is typically a modern way of thinking which is always looking outward and blaming everything around oneself. Perhaps this is the influence of the modern materialistic outlook of life. Materials are everything for a materialist who has no time to think what he is. He always looks around him but never looks at himself.

Let us think of an instance that I stumbled over. That "I" becomes the most important factor. It is said in the Dhammapada:

> *"All that we are is the result of*
> *what we have thought;*

*it is founded on our thoughts,
it is made up of our thoughts.
If a man speaks or acts with
a pure thought, happiness follows him,
like a shadow that never leaves him.
He abused me, he beat me,
he defeated me, he robbed me;
in those who do not harbor such thoughts
hatred will cease."*

ABOUT THE AUTHOR

Masao Kubose was born in San Francisco, California on June 21, 1905. He received his primary and secondary education in Hiroshima, Japan. After returning to the United States, he graduated from the University of California at Berkeley in 1935, majoring in philosophy. He then went to Japan and became a disciple of Reverend Haya Akegarasu with whom he studied for five years. He was ordained as a Shin Buddhist minister and given the Dharma name "Gyomay" which means "Bright Dawn."

Reverend Kubose returned to the United States in 1941. During World War II he was in a relocation camp in Heart Mountain, Wyoming. In 1944 he relocated to Chicago and founded the Buddhist Temple of Chicago as an independent religious organization with no administrative ties to any higher headquarters. His mission was to make Buddhism available to all Americans by presenting the teachings in non-sectarian, non-dualistic terminology. He is considered a pioneer in the Americanization of Buddhism, establishing the American Buddhist Association in 1955.

Reverend Kubose returned to Japan in 1966 to study Buddhism at Otani University in Kyoto and earned an M.A. degree. During this time he also studied and practiced Zen Buddhism. Upon his return to the United States in 1969, he established a meditation group and also a Buddhist Educational Center.

Reverend Kubose lectured widely all across the United States and abroad. He was honored many times for his work in the field of brotherhood and community relations. In 1971 he received the prestigious World Buddhist Mission Cultural Award from Yehan Numata's Bukkyo Dendo Kyokai. In 1987, he became the recipient of the 5th Class Order of the Sacred Treasure of Gold and Silver Rays from His Majesty the Emperor of Japan. Throughout his life, he emphasized and taught non-sectarian Buddha Dharma for all. Reverend Gyomay M. Kubose passed away on March 29, 2000 at the age of 94. Today in Chicago, an honorary street sign reads "Rev. Gyomay and Minnie Kubose Way" at the corner of Leland and Racine Avenues.

BOOKS BY GYOMAY M. KUBOSE

Everyday Suchness

Center Within

American Buddhism

Zen Koans

Fundamental Spirit of Buddhism
(Translation)

Heart of the Great Wisdom Sutra
(Translation and commentary)

Tan Butsu Ge
(Translation and commentary)

Above books and more are available from:

Dharma House Publishing

28372 Margaret Road, Coarsegold, CA 93614

www.brightdawn.org

info@brightdawn.org

www.ingramcontent.com/pod-product-compliance
Lightning Source LLC
Chambersburg PA
CBHW040552010526
44110CB00054B/2651